ANNIHILATION OF CASTE

Dr Bhimrao Ramji Ambedkar

Bhimrao Ramji Ambedkar 14 April 1891 - 6 December - 1956), also known as Babasaheb Ambedkar, was an Indian jurist, economist, politician and social reformer, who inspired the Dalit Buddhist movement and campaigned against social discrimination towards the untouchables (Dalits). He was a member of the Constituent Drafting committee. He was independent India's first Minister of Law and Justice, and considered the chief architect of the Constitution of India. Ambedkar was a prolific student, earning doctorates in economics from both Columbia University and the University of London, and gaining reputation as a scholar for his research in law, economics and political science.[13] In his early career, he was an economist, professor, and lawyer. His later life was marked by his political activities; he became involved in campaigning and negotiations for India's independence, publishing journals, advocating political rights and social freedom for Dalits, and contributing significantly to the establishment of the state of India. In 1956, he converted to Buddhism, initiating mass conversions of Dalits.

Published by IndiePress, an imprint of Westland Books, a division of Nasadiya Technologies Private Limited, in 2024

No. 269/2B, First Floor, 'Irai Arul', Vimalraj Street, Nethaji Nagar, Alapakkam Main Road, Maduravoyal, Chennai 600095

Westland, the Westland logo, IndiePress and the IndiePress logo are the trademarks of Nasadiya Technologies Private Limited, or its affiliates.

IndiePress Classics

IndiePress

ISBN: 978-93-6045-752-5

10 9 8 7 6 5 4 3 2 1

Typeset by MAP Systems, Bengaluru

Cover Designed by Malik

Publishing Manager: Jayantika Bajpai

Contents

Annihilation of Caste

Annihilation of Caste

Know truth as truth and untruth as untruth.
—Buddha

He that will not reason is a bigot. He that cannot reason is a fool. He that dare not reason is a slave—H. Drummond

Preface To The Second Edition, 1937

The speech prepared by me for the Jat-Pat Todak Mandal[b] of Lahore has had an astonishingly warm reception from the Hindu public for whom it was primarily intended. The English edition of one thousand five hundred copies was exhausted within two months of its publication. It has been translated into Gujarati and Tamil. It is being translated into Marathi, Hindi, Punjabi and Malayalam. The demand for the English text still continues unabated. To satisfy this demand it has become necessary to issue a second edition. Considerations of history and effectiveness of appeal have led me to retain the original form of the essay—namely, the speech form—although I was asked to recast it in the form of a direct narrative.

To this edition I have added two appendices. I have collected in Appendix I the two articles written by Mr Gandhi by way of review of my speech in the Harijan,[c] and his letter to Mr Sant Ram,[d] a member of the Jat-Pat Todak Mandat[e]

In Appendix II, I have printed my views in reply to the articles of Mr Gandhi collected in Appendix I. Besides Mr Gandhi, many others have adversely criticised my views as expressed in my speech. But I have felt that in taking notice of such adverse comments, I should limit myself to Mr Gandhi. This I have done not because what he has said is so weighty as to deserve a reply, but because to many a Hindu he is an oracle, so great that when he opens his lips it is expected that the argument must close and no dog must bark.

But the world owes much to rebels who would dare to argue in the face of the pontiff and insist that he is not infallible. I do not care for the credit which every progressive society must give to its rebels. I shall be satisfied if I make the Hindus realise that they are the sick men of India, and that their sickness is causing danger to the health and happiness of other Indians.

B.R. Ambedkar

Preface To The Third Edition, 1944

The second edition of this essay appeared in 1937, and was exhausted within a very short period. A new edition has been in demand for a long time. It was my intention to recast the essay so as to incorporate into it another essay of mine called "Castes in India: Their Mechanism, Genesis and Development," which appeared in the issue of the Indian Antiquary journal for May 1917.[f] But as I could not find time, and as there is very little prospect of my being able to do so, and as the demand for it from the public is very insistent, I am content to let this be a mere reprint of the second edition.

I am glad to find that this essay has become so popular, and I hope that it will serve the purpose for which it was intended.

B.R. Ambedkar 22, Prithviraj Road
New Delhi
1 December 1944

Prologue

On 12 December 1935,[g] I received the following letter from Mr Sant Ram, the secretary of the Jat-Pat Todak Mandal:

My dear Doctor Saheb,

Many thanks for your kind letter of the 5th December. I have released it for press without your permission for which I beg your pardon, as I saw no harm in giving it publicity. You are a great thinker, and it is my well-considered opinion that none else has studied the problem of caste so deeply as you have. I have always benefited myself and our Mandal from your ideas. I have explained and preached it in the Krantih many times and I have even lectured on it in many conferences. I am now very anxious to read the exposition of your new formula—"It is not possible to break caste without annihilating the religious notions on which it, the caste system, is founded." Please do explain it at length at your earliest convenience, so that we may take up the idea and emphasise it from press and platform. At present, it is not fully clear to me.

Our executive committee persists in having you as our president for our annual conference. We can change our dates to accommodate your convenience. Independent Harijansi of Punjab are very much desirous to meet you and discuss with you their plans. So if you kindly accept our request and come to Lahore to preside over the conference it will serve double purpose. We will invite Harijan leaders of all shades of opinion and you will get an opportunity of giving your ideas to them.

The Mandal has deputed our assistant secretary, Mr Indra Singh, to meet you at Bombay in Xmas and discuss with you the whole situation with a view to persuade you to please accept our request.

The Jat-Pat Todak Mandal is, I was given to understand, an organisation of caste-Hindu social reformers, with the one and only aim, namely, to eradicate the caste system from amongst the Hindus. As a rule, I do not like to take any part in a movement which is carried on by caste Hindus. Their attitude towards social reform is so different from mine that I have found it difficult to pull on with them. Indeed, I find their company quite uncongenial to me on account of our differences of opinion. Therefore when the Mandal first approached me, I declined their invitation to preside. The Mandal, however, would not take a refusal from me, and sent down one of its members to Bombay to press me to accept the invitation. In the end I agreed to preside. The annual conference was to be held at Lahore, the headquarters of the Mandal. The conference was to meet at Easter, but was subsequently postponed to the middle of May 1936.[j]

The reception committee of the Mandal has now cancelled the conference. The notice of cancellation came long after my presidential address had been printed. The copies of this address are now lying with me. As I did not get an opportunity to deliver the address from the presidential chair, the public has not had an opportunity to know my views on the problems created by the caste system.

To let the public know them, and also to dispose of the printed copies which are lying on my hand, I have decided to put the printed copies of the address in the market. The accompanying pages contain the text of that address.

The pubic will be curious to know what led to the cancellation of my appointment as the president of the conference. At the start, a dispute arose over the printing of the address. I desired that the address should be printed in Bombay. The Mandal wished that it should be printed in Lahore, on the grounds of economy. I did not agree, and insisted upon having it printed in Bombay. Instead of their agreeing to my proposition, I received a letter signed by several members of the Mandal, from which I give the following extract:

27 March 1936 Revered Doctor ji,

Your letter of the 24th instant addressed to Sjt. Sant Ramk has been shown to us. We were a little disappointed to read it. Perhaps you are not fully aware of the situation that has arisen here. Almost all the Hindus in the Punjab are against your being invited to this province. The Jat-Pat Todak Mandal has been subjected to the bitterest criticism and has received censorious rebuke from all quarters. All the Hindu leaders among whom being Bhai Parmanand, MLA (ex-president, Hindu Mahasabha),[1] Mahatma Hans Raj, Dr Gokal Chand Narang, minister for local self-government, Raja Narendra Nadym MLC etc., have dissociated themselves from this step of the Mandal.

Despite all this the runners of the Jat-Pat Todak Mandal (the leading figure being Sjt. Sant Ram) are determined to wade through thick and thin but would not give up the idea of your presidentship. The Mandal has earned a bad name.

Under the circumstances it becomes your duty to cooperate with the Mandal. On the one hand, they are being put to so much trouble and hardship by the Hindus, and if on the other hand you too augment their difficulties it will be a most sad coincidence of bad luck for them.

We hope you will think over the matter and do what is good for us all.

This letter puzzled me greatly. I could not understand why the Mandal should displease me, for the sake of a few rupees, in the matter of printing the address. Secondly, I could not believe that men like Sir Gokal Chand Narang had really resigned as a protest against my selection as president, because I had received the following letter from Sir Gokal Chand himself:

5. Montgomery Road, Lahore 7 February 1936

Dear Doctor Ambedkar,
I am glad to learn from the workers of the Jat-Pat Todak Mandal that you have agreed to preside at their next anniversary to be held at Lahore during the Easter holidays. It will give me much pleasure if you stay with me while you are at Lahore.

More when we meet.
Yours sincerelv,
G.C. Narang

Whatever be the truth, I did not yield to this pressure. But even when the Mandal found that I was insisting upon having my address printed in Bombay, instead of agreeing to my proposal the Mandal sent me a wire that they were sending Mr Har Bhagwann to Bombay to "talk over matters personally". Mr Har Bhagwan came to Bombay on the 9th of April. When I met Mr Har Bhagwan, I found that he had nothing to say regarding the issue. Indeed he was so unconcerned regarding the printing of the address—whether it should be printed in Bombay or in Lahore—that he did not even mention it in the course of our conversation.

All that he was anxious for was to know the contents of the address. I was then convinced that in getting the address printed in Lahore, the main object of the Mandal was not to save money but to get at the contents of the address. I gave him a copy. He did not feel very happy with some parts of it. He returned to Lahore. From Lahore, he wrote to me the following letter:

Lahore, 14 April 1936 My dear Doctor Saheb,

Since my arrival from Bombay, on the 12th, I have been indisposed owing to my having not slept continuously for five or six nights, which were spent in the train. Reaching here I came to know that you had come to Amritsar. o I would have seen you there if I were well enough to go about. I have made over your address to Mr Sant Ram for translation and he has liked it very much, but he is not sure whether it could be translated by him for printing before the 25th. In any case, it would have a wide publicity and we are sure it would wake the Hindus up from their slumber.

The passage I pointed out to you at Bombay has been read by some of our friends with a little misgiving, and those of us who would like to see the conference terminate without any untoward incident would prefer that at least the word "Veda" be left out for the time being. I leave this to your good sense. I hope, however, in your concluding paragraphs you will make it clear that the views expressed in the address are your own and that the responsibility does not lie on the Mandal. I hope you will not mind this statement of mine and would let us have 1,000 copies of the address, for which we shall, of course, pay. To this effect I have sent you a telegram today. A cheque of Rs 100 is enclosed herewith which kindly acknowledge, and send us your bills in due time.

I have called a meeting of the reception committee and shall communicate their decision to you immediately. In the meantime kindly accept my heartfelt thanks for the kindness shown to me and the great pains taken by you in the preparation of your address. You have really put us under a heavy debt of gratitude.

Yours sincerely, Har Bhagwan

P.S.: Kindly send the copies of the address by passenger train as soon as it is printed, so that copies may be sent to the press for publication.

Accordingly I handed over my manuscript to the printer with an order to print thousand copies.

Eight days later, I received another letter from Mr Har Bhagwan which I reproduce below:

Lahore, 22 April 1936 Dear Dr Ambedkar,

We are in receipt of your telegram and letter, for which kindly accept our thanks. In accordance with your desire, we have again postponed our conference, but feel that it would have been much better to have it on the 25th and 26th, as the weather is growing warmer and warmer every day in the Punjab. In the middle of May it would be fairly hot, and the sittings in the daytime would not be very pleasant and comfortable. However, we shall try our best to do all we can to make things as comfortable as possible, if it is held in the middle of May.

There is, however, one thing that we have been compelled to bring to your kind attention. You will remember that when I pointed out to you the misgivings entertained by some of our people regarding your declaration on the subject of change of religion,[p] you told me that it was undoubtedly outside the scope of the Mandal and that you had no intention to say anything from our platform in that connection. At the same time when the manuscript of your address was handed to me you assured me that that was the main portion of your address and that there were only two or three concluding paragraphs that you wanted to add. On receipt of the second instalment of your address we have been taken by surprise, as that would make it so lengthy, that we are afraid very few people would read the whole of it. Besides that you have more than once stated in your address that you had decided to walk out of the fold of the Hindus and that that was your last address a Hindu. You have also unnecessarily attacked the morality and reasonableness of the Vedas and other religious books of the Hindus, and have at length dwelt upon the technical side of Hindu religion, which has absolutely no connection with the problem at issue, so much so that some of the passages have become irrelevant and off the point. We would have been very pleased if you had confined your address to that portion given to me, or if an addition was necessary, it would have been limited to what you had written on Brahminism, etc. The last portion which deals with the complete annihilation of the Hindu religion and doubts the morality of the sacred books of the Hindus as well as a hint about your intention to leave the Hindu fold does not seem to me to be relevant.

I would therefore most humbly request you on behalf of the people responsible for the conference to leave out the passages referred to above, and close the address with what was given to me or add a few paragraphs on Brahminism. We doubt the wisdom of making the address unnecessarily provocative and pinching. There are several of us who subscribe to your feelings and would very much want to be under your banner for remodelling the Hindu religion. If you had decided to get together persons of your cult, I can assure you a large number would have joined your army of reformers from the Punjab.

In fact, we thought you would give us a lead in the destruction of the evil of [the] caste system, especially when you have studied the subject so thoroughly, and strengthen our hands by bringing about a revolution and making yourself as a nucleus in the gigantic effort, but [a] declaration of the nature made by you, when repeated, loses its power, and becomes a hackneyed term. Under the circumstances, I would request you to consider the whole matter and make your address more effective by saying that you would be glad to take a leading part in the destruction of the caste system if the Hindus are willing to work in right earnest towards that end, even if they had to forsake their kith and kin and the religious notions. In case you do so, I am sanguine that you would find a ready response from the Punjab in such an endeavour.

I shall be grateful if you will help us at this juncture as we have already undergone much expenditure and have been put to suspense, and let us know by the return of post that you have condescended to limit your address as above. In case you still insist upon the printing of the address in toto, we very much regret it would not be possible—rather advisable—for us to hold the conference, and would prefer to postpone it sine die, although by doing so we shall be losing the goodwill of the people because of the repeated postponements. We should, however, like to point out that you have carved a niche in our hearts by writing such a wonderful treatise on the caste system, which excels all other treatises so far written and will prove to be a valuable heritage, so to say. We shall be ever indebted to you for the pains taken by you in its preparation.

Thanking you very much for your kindness and with best wishes.

I am yours sincerely, Har Bhagwan

To this letter I sent the following reply: 27 April 1936

Dear Mr Har Bhagwan,
I am in receipt of your letter of the 22nd April. I note with regret that the reception committee of the Jat-Pat Todak Mandal "would prefer to postpone the conference sine die" if I insisted upon printing the address in toto. In reply I have to inform you that I also would prefer to have the conference cancelled—I do not like to use vague terms—if the Mandal insisted upon having my address pruned to suit its circumstances. You may not like my decision. But I cannot give up, for the sake of the honour of presiding over the conference,[q] the liberty which every president must have in the preparation of the address. I cannot give up, for the sake of pleasing the Mandal, the duty which every president owes to the conference over which he presides, to give it a lead which he thinks right and proper. The issue is one of principle, and I feel I must do nothing to compromise it in any way.

I would not have entered into any controversy as regards the propriety of the decision taken by the reception committee. But as you have given certain reasons which appear to throw the blame on me, I am bound to answer them. In the first place, I must dispel the notion that the views contained in that part of the address to which objection has been taken by the committee have come to the Mandal as a surprise. Mr Sant Ram, I am sure, will bear me out when I say that in reply to one of his letters I had said that the real method of breaking up the caste system was not to bring about inter-caste dinners and inter-caste marriages but to destroy the religious notions on which caste was founded, and that Mr Sant Ram in return asked me to explain what he said was a novel point of view. It was in response to this invitation from Mr Sant Ram that I thought I ought to elaborate in my address what I had stated in a sentence in my letter to him. You cannot, therefore, say that the views expressed are new. At any rate, they are not new to Mr Sant Ram, who is the moving spirit and the leading light of your Mandal. But I go further and say that I wrote this part of my address not merely because I felt it desirable to do so. I wrote it because I thought that it was absolutely necessary to complete the argument. I am amazed to read that you characterise the portion of the speech to which your committee objects as "irrelevant and off the point". You will allow me to say that I am a lawyer and I know the rules of relevancy as well as any member of your committee. I most emphatically maintain that the portion objected to is not only most relevant but is also most important. It is in that part of the address that I have discussed the ways and means of breaking up the caste system. It may be that the conclusion I have arrived at as to the best method of destroying caste is startling and painful. You are entitled to say that my analysis is wrong. But you cannot say that in an address which deals with the problem of caste it is not open to me to discuss how caste can be destroyed.

Your other complaint relates to the length of the address. I have pleaded guilty to the charge in the address itself. But who is really responsible for this? I fear you have come rather late on the scene. Otherwise you would have known that originally I had planned to write a short address, for my own convenience, as I had neither the time nor the energy to engage myself in the preparation of an elaborate thesis. It was the Mandal which asked me to deal with the subject exhaustively, and it was the Mandal which sent down to me a list of questions relating to the caste system and asked me to answer them in the body of my address, as they were questions which were often raised in the controversy between the Mandal and its opponents, and which the Mandal found difficult to answer satisfactorily.

It was in trying to meet the wishes of the Mandal in this respect that the address has grown to the length to which it has. In view of what I have said, I am sure you will agree that the fault respecting the length of the address is not mine.

I did not expect that your Mandal would be so upset because I have spoken of the destruction of the Hindu religion. I thought it was only fools who were afraid of words. But lest there should be any misapprehension in the minds of the people, I have taken great pains to explain what I mean by religion and destruction of religion. I am sure that nobody, on reading my address, could possibly misunderstand me. That your Mandal should have taken a fright at mere words as "destruction of religion, etc.", notwithstanding the explanation that accompanies them, does not raise the Mandal in my estimation. One cannot have any respect or regard for men who take the position of the reformer and then refuse even to see the logical consequences of that position, let alone following them out in action.

You will agree that I have never accepted to be limited in any way in the preparation of my address, and the question as to what the address should or should not contain was never even discussed between myself and the Mandal. I had always taken for granted that I was free to express in the address such views as I held on the subject. Indeed, until you came to Bombay on the 9th April, the Mandal did not know what sort of an address I was preparing. It was when you came to Bombay that I voluntarily told you that I had no desire to use your platform from which to advocate my views regarding change of religion by the Depressed Classes. I think I have scrupulously kept that promise in the preparation of the address. Beyond a passing reference of an indirect character where I say that "I am sorry I will not be here, etc.", I have said nothing about the subject in my address. When I see you object even to such a passing and so indirect a reference, I feel bound to ask, did you think that in agreeing to preside over your conference I would be agreeing to suspend or to give up my views regarding change of faith by the Depressed Classes? If you did think so, I must tell you that I am in no way responsible for such a mistake on your part. If any of you had even hinted to me that in exchange for the honour you were doing me by electing [me] as president, I was to abjure my faith in my programme of conversion, I would have told you in quite plain terms that I cared more for my faith than for any honour from you.

After your letter of the 14th, this letter of yours comes as a surprise to me. I am sure that anyone who reads them both will feel the same. I cannot account for this sudden volte-face on the part of the reception committee. There is no difference in substance between the rough draft which was before the committee when you wrote your letter of the 14th, and the final draft on which the decision of the committee communicated to me in your letter under reply was taken. You cannot point out a single new idea in the final draft which is not contained in the earlier draft. The ideas are the same. The only difference is that they have been worked out in greater detail in the final draft. If there was anything to object to in the address, you could have said so on the 14th. But you did not. On the contrary, you asked me to print off 1,000 copies, leaving me the liberty to accept or not the verbal changes which you suggested. Accordingly I got 1,000 copies printed, which are now lying with me. Eight days later you write to say that you object to the address and that if it is not amended the conference will be cancelled. You ought to have known that there was no hope of any alteration being made in the address. I told you when you were in Bombay that I would not alter a comma, that I would not allow any censorship over my address, and that you would have to accept the address as it came from me. I also told you that the responsibility for the views expressed in the address was entirely mine, and if they were not liked by the conference I would not mind at all if the conference passed a resolution condemning them. So anxious was I to relieve your Mandal from having to assume responsibility for my views—and also with the object of not getting myself entangled by too intimate an association with your conference—I suggested to you that I desired to have my address treated as a sort of an inaugural address and not as a presidential address, and that the Mandal should find someone else to preside over the conference and deal with the resolutions. Nobody could have been better placed to take a decision on the 14th than your committee. The committee failed to do that, and in the meantime cost of printing has been incurred which, I am sure, with a little more firmness on the part of your committee, could have been saved.

I feel sure that the views expressed in my address have little to do with the decision of your committee. I have reason to believe that my presence at the Sikh Prachar Conference held at Amritsar has had a good deal to do with the decision of the committee. Nothing else can satisfactorily explain the sudden volte-face shown by the committee between the 14th and the 22nd April. I must not, however, prolong this controversy, and must request you to announce immediately that the session of the conference which was to meet under my presidentship is cancelled. All the grace has by now run out, and I shall not consent to preside, even if your committee agreed to accept my address as it is, in toto. I thank you for your appreciation of the pains I have taken in the preparation of the address. I certainly have profited by the labour, if no one else does. My only regret is that I was put to such hard labour at a time when my health was not equal to the strain it has caused.

Yours sincerely,
B.R. Ambedkar

This correspondence will disclose the reasons which have led to the cancellation by the Mandal of my appointment as president, and the reader will be in a position to lay the blame where it ought properly to belong. This is I believe the first time when the appointment of a president is cancelled by the reception committee because it does not approve of the views of the president. But whether that is so or not, this is certainly the first time in my life to have been invited to preside over a conference of caste Hindus. I am sorry that it has ended in a tragedy. But what can anyone expect from a relationship so tragic as the relationship between the reforming sect of caste Hindus and the self-respecting sect of Untouchables, where the former have no desire to alienate their orthodox fellows, and the latter have no alternative but to insist upon reform being carried out?

B.R. Ambedkar Rajgriha,

Dadar Bombay-14

15 May 1936

Notes

a. These epigraphs were added by Ambedkar to the title page of the 1937 edition. The quote from Buddha is from Verse 12 of The Dhammapada and Sutta Nipata (p.3), part of Sacred Books of the East, Vol. 10 by Max Müller and Max Fausböll (1881). Drummond's words are derived from the last lines from his preface to Academical Questions, Vol. 1 (1805, xv). Sir William Drummond (not H. Drummond as erroneously printed in the 1937 edition) was a Scottish diplomat and Member of Parliament, poet and philosopher. Ambedkar amends the punctuation and wording of Drummond's words which read: "He, who will not reason, is a bigot; he, who cannot, is a fool; he, who dares not, is a slave."

b. The Jat-Pat Todak Mandal (Forum for the Break-up of Caste) was a radical faction of the Arya Samaj, a Hindu reformist organisation that was founded in Lahore on 10 April 1875 by Swami Dayananda Saraswati (1824–83). According to Sant Ram (see Note 3), in November 1922, about twenty- two men and women, at the behest of Arya Samaj leader Bhai Parmanand, met at his Lahore residence with the objective of forming a separate outfit to fight caste. In his autobiography Mere jivan ke anubhav (Experiences of my life, 1963/2008), Sant Ram says he suggested the name Jat-Pat Todak Mandal. The eighteen founding members of the Mandal listed by Sant Ram are: Bhai Parmanand (president); Pandit Bhoomand; Pandit Paramanand, B.A.; Chowdhary Kanhaiyalal; Babu Teertharam, cotton factory owner; Chak Jhumra; Pandit Brahmadatt Vidyalankar of Delhi; Shri Sudarshan, shortstory writer; Pandit Dharmadev; Deewanchand, officebearer of Arya Samaj, Jalandhar; Pandit Sant Ram, priest and Arya Samaj worker of Nau Shehra; Paramanand Arya, coal company, Lahore; Pandit Chetram, teacher, Girls School, Jalandhar; Devnath of Gurudutt Bhavan, Lahore; Devamitra, M.Sc., of Gurudutt Bhavan, Lahore; Dharmendra Nath, M.A., of Meerut; Sant Ram, B.A.; Mrs Parvati, wife of Pandit Bhoomanand; Mrs Subhadra Devi, wife of Pandit Paramanand. From the names, it appears that 'Untouchables' were not part of this distinctly caste-Hindu initiative, a point that Ambedkar draws our attention to in the Prologue of this address (p.189). The Mandal insisted on inter-dining and intermarriage. Membership, on paying two rupees as annual subscription, was meant for Hindus who took a vow to marry themselves or their children out of their caste.

c. Following his fallout with Ambedkar over the Communal Award of 1932 and the signing of the Poona Pact (see "A Note on the Poona Pact", in this book, 357–76), M.K.

Gandhi launched the Harijan Sevak Sangh in 1932 and an English weekly named Harijan in 1933. Ambedkar preferred the term Untouchable, with capitals, or the official term, Depressed Classes. He also preferred to address those within the varna fold as "caste Hindus" or savarnas, and sometimes as Touchables.

d. Sant Ram B.A., one of the founder-members of the Jat-Pat Todak Mandal, was born on 14 Februar 1887 in Puranibassi, Hoshiarpur district, Punjab. In his autobiography, he (1963/2008, 12) says the Gohil surname his father carried was found among Rajputs (warriors), Banias (traders) and Kumhars (potters). Sant Ram always used his graduation degree—B.A.—as initials to disavow caste-related surnames, though he identifies himself as a Kumhar. However, one source says he was born into the Megh caste, listed as a Scheduled Caste in today's Punjab (Kshirsagar 1994, 323). Sant Ram says that Kumhars in his village did not make pots but practised trade. Sant Ram's father, Ramdas Gohil, the first person in the village to educate his children, acquired wealth and influence through trade which took him as far away as Central Asia. Sant Ram was married at the age of twelve to an unlettered girl whom he taught to read and write and brought out of purdah. Five years after his first wife died, in 1929, according to the journal The Indian Rationalist (1952), he married "Sundar Bai Proothan, a Maharashtrian virgin widow. The marriage was notable for three reasons: it was a widow marriage, an intercaste marriage, and an inter-provincial marriage." Sundar Bai had been rendered a child widow at the age of eight. Sant Ram recounts two instances of caste discrimination, the first when studying in fourth grade in Ambala and the second when at college in Lahore at the hands of Banias, the merchant caste. In 1930, he published Phansi ke pujari (Priests of the noose) in Urdu, featuring biographies of nationalists, entitled Inquilab ke parvane (Moths to the flame of revolution) on the inside title page. A 1947 partition refugee, Sant Ram died in New Delhi in 1998 at the age of 101. In one of his exchanges with the Mandal featured in the Prologue, Ambedkar describes Sant Ram as the "moving spirit and the leading light" of the Mandal (p.199).

e. In 1931, the Mandal campaigned against the declaration of caste in the census. Mark Juergensmeye (1982/2009, 39) writes that the Mandal relied heavily on the support of privileged-caste Arya Samajis in this regard. This may have caused the Mandal to refuse the address prepared by Ambedkar. Bhai Parmanand was the first president and he continued to support the Mandal despite the rift in 1924 when its permission to use the Arya Samaj pandal was revoked.

f. For an annotated edition of "Castes in India", see Rege (2013). Indian Antiquary was an Orientali monthly founded in 1872 by Dr James Burgess. It provided a platform for scholarly articles by both European and Indian scholars. In full, it was called The Indian Antiquary: A Journal of Oriental Research in Archaeology, Epigraphy, Ethnology, Geography, History, Folklore, Languages, Literature, Numismatics, Philosophy, Religion, Etc.

g. The portion of the Prologue from here till the end of Sant Ram's letter has been added in the 1937 edition.

h. Kranti (Revolution), edited by Sant Ram, was an Urdu monthly published from Lahore. After the founding of the Jat-Pat Todak Mandal, Sant Ram (1963/2008, 116) says the forum tried publishing a monthly magazine in Hindi. A monthly eight-page broadsheet called Jat-Pat Todak, priced at Rs 1.50, was published from December

1922 to September 1924, but it failed owing to the lack of Hindi readers. The Mandal produced, for free distribution, many books in Hindi, Urdu and English on the question of caste. In January 1927, Jat-Pat Todak was revived, this time as an Urdu publication. In January 1928, this was renamed Kranti, with Sant Ram as chief editor. "This became a very popular magazine," according to Sant Ram. "Produced in Royal Octavo size, it had 64 pages. The magazine's Health Special, Children's Special, Women's Special, and Men's Special were extremely popular ... Since the Mandal's key assets were stuck in Pakistan, Kranti folded up after its last issue in August 1947 ... After a gap, we revived it for two or three issues in India. Since the conditions were not right, we lost about Rs 2,000 and shut down Kranti for good" (117). According to Bhagwan Das (2010a, 21—2), Kranti was the only Urdu magazine that reported on the speeches of Ambedkar. Das also mentions the Mandal's strong aversion to the conversion of Untouchables due to its proximity to the Arya Samaj.

i. Harijan, 'children of god', was the epithet used by M.K. Gandhi, beginning 1932, to paternalistica refer to 'Untouchables'. The term figures in the bhajan "Vaishnava jana to" by Narsinh Mehta (1414?—1481?), a Gujarati Brahmin Vaishnavite poet-saint, which was popularised by Gandhi. The scholar Aishwary Kumar (2014) draws our attention to Gandhi citing Tulsidas's sixteenth- century Ramayana, one of his favourite books on this term: "You know the word 'Harijan' occurs in Tulsidas's Ramayana? There Lakshmana describes to Parashurama the characteristic of a true Kshatriya. He says: (It is the trait of our clan never to use force towards a god, a Brahmin, a Harijan or a cow)" (CWMG 68, 327). The British government, from 1916 onwards, deployed the bureaucratic term Depressed Classes (used first in the volumes of the Bombay Gazetteer in 1877), which was replaced by Scheduled Castes in 1935 by the Government of India Act—a term that continues to be used in official parlance till date. 'Harijan' has been steadfasdy rejected by the Ambedkarite and Dalit movements. Though the founding of the militant organisation Dalit Panther in Bombay in 1972 gave an all-India currency to Dalit (broken, crushed people), the term has been used in western India in this sense at least since Jotiba Phule's (1827–90) time. Phule is supposed to have used Dalit in terms of dalittuthan (uplift of the downtrodden), but the evidence is anecdotal (Louis 2003, 144). Phule used the term Ati-Shudra for Untouchables in his writings. Etymologically, the origins of the term Dalit can be traced to the Buddha's usage of the Pali dalidda in the Dalidda Sutta, said to have been preached at the Kalandakanivapa in Rajagaha (Samyutta Nikaya: XI.14). In Pali Buddhist literature, the term dalidda (daridra in Sanskrit) is used for the property-less poor in contrast to the gahapati class of the rich. Nalin Swaris (2011, 99), citing Anguttara Nikaya: 111.84, says: "The dalidda-kula, the pauper-lineage, is described as people without enough to eat and drink, without even a covering for their back." More recently, the Dalit leader P.N. Rajbhoj founded the journal Dalit Bandhu (Friend of Dalits) in Pune in 1928. For an account of the nascent histories of the terms Untouchable, Depressed Classes, Harijan, Scheduled Caste, etc., see Simon Charsley (1996). Sant Ram's use of the term Harijan here shows how within three years of Gandhi coining the term it had entrenched itself among reformers and intellectuals. As Ambedkar says in the very opening paragraph of AoC, "I have questioned the authority of the Mahatma whom they [the Mandal] revere".

j. In the process of opening with Sant Ram's letter in the 1937 edition, Ambedkar rearranges the contents of this paragraph without affecting its import.

k. Sjt. here is short for the respectful prefix 'Srijut', commonly used during this period. For instance, Gandhi's autobiography the prefix Sjt. is often used (such as Sjt. Vitthalbhai Patel). The 1931 Macmillan edition of Mahatma Gandhi: His Own Story edited by C.F. Andrews has a glossary page that explains Srijut as "a common title the equivalent to 'Esquire'".

l. Bhai Parmanand (1876–1947) wore many hats. Born in Lahore, he started as an Arya Samaji unde the influence of Lala Lajpat Rai and Lala Har Dayal, and moved to the far right as a Vedic missionary of the Samaj, travelling the world (South Africa, Guyana, Martinique, the US, South America) preaching, and became a founder-member of the Ghadar Party that sought to overthrow British rule. Remembered today for his leadership of the Hindu Mahasabha and for being a proponent of Hindutva, he was sentenced in 1915 to imprisonment on the Andamans in the First Lahore Conspiracy Case. Parmanand is also regarded as the first advocate of an Islamic state divided out of the subcontinent. Following the British announcement of the partition of Bengal in 1905, he suggested that "the territory beyond Sindh should be united with Afghanistan and North-West Frontier Province into a great Musulman Kingdom. The Hindus of the region should come away, while at the same time the Musulmans in the rest of the country should go and settle in this territory" (cited in Yadav and Arya 1988, 196). Also see Parmanand's autobiography translated into English, The Story of My Life (1934/2003). Jaffrelot (2010, 139) cites Parmanand's 1936 work,

Hindu Sangathan, where he excoriates the Buddha for attacking the varnashrama system: "The abolition of castes and ashrams cut at the very root of social duties. How could a nation hope to live after having lost sight of this aspect of Dharma? 'Equality for all' is an appealing abstraction; but the nation could not long survive the rejection or destruction of Dharma." Parmanand espouses such views in the year of inviting Ambedkar, and even as he is the founder- president of the Jat-Pat Todak Mandal.

m. Mahatma Hans Raj was among the first wave of a young, new generation of educated Hindus joini the Arya Samaj. Later he became the principal of the Dayanand Anglo-Vedic College, Lahore, over which he presided from 1888 to 1911. Gokal Chand Narang belonged to the DAV (College) faction of the Arya Samaj and acquired influence alongside the rich landowner, Raja Narendra Nath, in the Legislative Assembly opposed to the encroachment of the Congress in the Punjab. For a history of the Arya Samaj and its leaders, see Kenneth W. Jones (1976).

n. Har Bhagwan's full name, according to the journal The Atheist (March-April 1974), was Har Bhagwan Sethi. He may have given up his (Bania) caste surname owing to his membership of the Jat-Pat Todak Mandal; he served as its secretary at one time. As an associate of Sant Ram, he was "closely associated with the abolition of caste distinctions". He died in 1976 at the age of eight- one in Delhi, having emigrated after partition from Lahore like Sant Ram. Notably, Har Bhagwan was the publisher of Swami Dharmateertha's The Menace of Hindu Imperialism (1941). Dharmateertha, born Parameswara Menon, a Nair from Kerala, came under the influence of Sree Narayana Guru (1856—1928), the pioneering anticaste social reformer who preached the message of "one caste, one religion, one god". In 1937, Dharmateertha led "the life of a wandering sannyasin and spread the Guru's social message of castelessness and social egalitarianism across the sub-continent" (Aloysius 2004, 19). Aloysius cites Ambedkar's words on this work in the blurb of the new edition: "This book is written from a point of view which I appreciate very much. I am myself writing a book in which I have touched many of the points which I find are dealt with in this book. The book therefore was a very welcome thing to me." After touring much of North India, Dharmateertha settled down in Lahore for five years (1941—6) at Har Bhagwan's house, and as a member of the Indian Social Congress met and held discussions with Jinnah, Ambedkar and the Sikh leader Master Tara Singh. In a short account in The Atheist (1974), Har Bhagwan says that after moving to Delhi he founded the Jat-Pat Todak Samata Sangh (Association for Equality Without Caste) which was soon renamed Avarnodaya Samata Sangh (Association for the Advancement of Casteless People).

o. On 13—14 April 1936, Ambedkar attended the Sikh Prachar Conference in Amritsar (50 km from Lahore). In his address he extolled the principle of equality within the Sikh community and alluded to the possibility of converting to Sikhism. Zelliot (2013, 162) writes: "There is an unverified story that Ambedkar spoke to a Sikh group at this time, asking them if they were willing to allow inter-marriage between Sikhs and new converts, and the Sikhs responded in the affirmative." For an analysis of why Ambedkar gave up on Sikhism, see Puri (2003, 2698), who says: "After participating in the Sikh Missionary Conference at Amritsar in April, Ambedkar sent his son, Yashwant Rao, and nephew to the Golden Temple in May, where they stayed for one month and a half, to observe the situation and meet with leaders of the community." Puri argues that perhaps the Shiromani Gurdwara Parbandhak Committee (SGPC) feared that "after six crore (60 million) untouchables became Sikhs" the clout of dominant-caste Jats in the SGPC and the gurdwaras would be undermined.

p. This must be seen in the light of the statement Ambedkar had made on 13 October 1935 at the Yeol Depressed Classes conference: "I had the misfortune of being born with the stigma of an Untouchable. However, it is not my fault; but I will not die a Hindu, for this is in my power" (Zelliot 2013, 147). The conference was attended by ten thousand people, a conglomeration of Mahar panchayats and delegates from Hyderabad and the Central Provinces. "The conference included an instruction to stop temple entry movements and an exhortation to cease fruitless attempts to gain status on Hindu terms" (Zelliot 2013, 148). Sant Ram (1963/2008, 137) writes, "One of the reasons for my inviting Dr Ambedkar was that in matters we can't convince him with logic, we would convince him in love by appealing to his heart." Ambedkar's insistence on including in his address a detailed section on the destruction of the Hindu religion signalled the likelihood of failure if the Mandal insisted on trying to win him over to the cause of religious reform. At the same time, members of the Mandal's welcome committee were threatened with a blackflag protest if Ambedkar were to preside over the meeting, and this made Sant Ram unsure of endearing Ambedkar to the cause. Ambedkar's address at the Sikh Prachar Conference, Amritsar, in April 1936 would have further disoriented the Jat- Pat Todak Mandal, a point Ambedkar makes in his final letter to the Mandal (203).

q. Sant Ram (1963/2008, 119), in his autobiography, lists the following past presidents of the Mandal's annual conferences in Lahore from a 1939 report of the Mandal: Swami Shraddhanand, Motilal Nehru, Raja Narendra Nath, Bhai Parmanand, Rameshwari Nehru, Swami Sarvadanand, Sir Hari Singh Gaur, Sri Satyananda Stokes, Sri Ramananda Chatterjee, Sri Harkishan Lal, Barrister Dr Gokul Chand, Barrister Dr N.B. Khare of Nagpur, Swami Satyanand and Dr Kalyandas Desai.

Annihilation of Caste

An Undelivered Speech, 1936

1

1.1

Friends, I am really sorry for the members of the Jat-Pat Todak Mandal who have so very kindly invited me to preside over this conference. I am sure they will be asked many questions for having selected me as the president. The Mandal will be asked to explain as to why it has imported a man from Bombay to preside over a function which is held in Lahore. I believe the Mandal could easily have found someone better qualified than myself to preside on the occasion. I have criticised the Hindus. I have questioned the authority of the Mahatma whom they revere. They hate me. To them I am a snake in their garden. The Mandal will no doubt be asked by the politically minded Hindus to explain why it has called me to fill this place of honour. It is an act of great daring. I shall not be surprised if some political Hindus regard it as an insult. This selection of mine certainly cannot please the ordinary religiously minded Hindus.

1.2

The Mandal may be asked to explain why it has disobeyed the shastric injunction in selecting the president. According to the shastras, the Brahmin is appointed to be the guru for the three varnas.[1] is a direction of the shastras. The Mandal therefore knows from whom a Hindu should take his lessons and from whom he should not. The shastras do not permit a Hindu to accept anyone as his guru merely because he is well versed. This is made very clear by Ramdas,[2] a Brahmin saint from Maharashtra, who is alleged to have inspired Shivaji to establish a Hindu Raj. In his Dasbodh, a socio-politicoreligious treatise in Marathi verse, Ramdas asks, addressing the Hindus, can we accept an antyaja[3] to be our guru because he is a pandit (i.e., learned)? He gives an answer in the negative.

1.3

What replies to give to these questions is a matter which I must leave to the Mandal. The Mandal knows best the reasons which led it to travel to Bombay to select a president, to fix upon a man so repugnant to the Hindus, and to descend so low in the scale as to select an antyaja—an Untouchable—to address an audience of the savarnas.[4] As for myself, you will allow me to say that I have accepted the invitation much against my will, and also against the will of many of my fellow Untouchables. I know that the Hindus are sick of me. I know that I am not a persona grata with them. Knowing all this, I have deliberately kept myself away from them. I have no desire to inflict myself upon them. I have been giving expression to my views from my own platform. This has already caused a great deal of heartburn[5] and irritation.

1.4

I have no desire to ascend the platform of the Hindus, to do within their sight what I have been doing within their hearing. If I am here it is because of your choice and not because of my wish. Yours is a cause of social reform. That cause has always made an appeal to me, and it is because of this that I felt I ought not to refuse an opportunity of helping the cause—especially when you think that I can help it. Whether what I am going to say today will help you in any way to solve the problem you are grappling with, is for you to judge. All I hope to do is to place before you my views on the problem.

2

2.1

The path of social reform, like the path to heaven (at any rate, in India), is strewn with many difficulties. Socialreform in India has few friends and many critics. The critics fall into two distinct classes. One class consists of political reformers, and the other of the socialists.

2.2

It was at one time recognised that without social efficiency,[6] no permanent progress in the other fields of activity was possible; that owing to mischief wrought by evil customs, Hindu society was not in a state of efficiency; and that ceaseless efforts must be made to eradicate these evils. It was due to the recognition of this fact that the birth of the National Congress was accompanied by the foundation of the Social Conference.[7] While the Congress was concerned with defining the weak points in the political organisation of the country, the Social Conference was engaged in removing the weak points in the social organisation of Hindu society. For some time the Congress and the Conference worked as two wings of one common activity, and they held their annual sessions in the same pandal.

2.3

But soon the two wings developed into two parties, a 'political reform party and a 'social reform party', between whom there raged a fierce controversy. The 'political reform party supported the National Congress, and the 'social reform party' supported the Social Conference. The two bodies thus became two hostile camps. The point at issue was whether social reform should precede political reform. For a decade the forces were evenly balanced, and the battle was fought without victory to either side.

2.4

It was, however, evident that the fortunes of the Social Conference were ebbing fast. The gentlemen who presided over the sessions of the Social Conference lamented that the majority of the educated Hindus were for political advancement and indifferent to social reform; and that while the number of those who attended the Congress was very large, and the number who did not attend but who sympathised with it was even larger, the number of those who attended the Social Conference was very much smaller.

2.5

This indifference—this thinning of its ranks—was soon followed by active hostility from the politicians. Under the leadership of the late Mr Tilak,[8] the courtesy with which the Congress allowed the Social Conference the use of its pandal was withdrawn, and the spirit of enmity went to such a pitch that when the Social Conference desired to erect its own pandal, a threat to burn the pandal was held out by its opponents.[9] Thus in the course of time the party in favour of political reform won, and the Social Conference vanished and was forgotten.

2.6

The speech delivered by Mr W.C. Bonnerjee[10] in 1892 at Allahabad, as president of the eighth session of the Congress, sounds like a funeral oration on the death of the Social Conference, and is so typical of the Congress attitude that I venture to quote from it the following extract. Mr Bonnerjee said:

I for one have no patience with those who say we shall not be fit for political reform until we reform our social system. I fail to see any connection between the two ... Are we not fit (for political reform) because our widows remain unmarried and our girls are given in marriage earlier than in other countries? ...because our wives and daughters do not drive about with us visiting our friends? ...because we do not send our daughters to Oxford and Cambridge? (Cheers from the audience)

2.7

I have stated the case for political reform as put by Mr Bonnerjee. There were many who were happy that the victory went to the Congress. But those who believe in the importance of social reform may ask, is an argument such as that of Mr Bonnerjee final? Does it prove that the victory went to those who were in the right? Does it prove conclusively that social reform has no bearing on political reform? It will help us to understand the matter if I state the other side of the case. I will draw upon the treatment of the Untouchables for my facts.

2.8

Under the rule of the Peshwas in the Maratha country,[11] the Untouchable was not allowed to use the public streets if a Hindu was coming along, lest he should pollute the Hindu by his shadow. The Untouchable was required to have a black thread either on his wrist or around his neck, as a sign or a mark to prevent the Hindus from getting themselves polluted by his touch by mistake. In Poona, the capital of the Peshwa, the Untouchable was required to carry, strung from his waist, a broom to sweep away from behind himself the dust he trod on, lest a Hindu walking on the same dust should be polluted. In Poona, the Untouchable was required to carry an earthen pot hung around his neck wherever he went—for holding his spit, lest his spit falling on the earth should pollute a Hindu who might unknowingly happen to tread on it.

2.9

Let me take more recent facts. The tyranny practised by the Hindus upon the Balais, an Untouchable community in Central India, will serve my purpose. You will find a report of this in the Times of India of 4th January 1928. The correspondent of the Times of India reported that high-caste Hindus— viz., Kalotas, Rajputs and Brahmins, including the Patels and Patwaris of the villages of Kanaria,

Bicholi-Hapsi, Bicholi- Mardana, and about fifteen other villages in Indore district (of Indore State)—informed the Balais of their respective villages that if they wished to live among them, they must conform to the following rules:

1. Balais must not wear gold-lace-bordered pugrees.
2. They must not wear dhotis with coloured or fancy borders.
3. They must convey intimation of the death of any Hindu to relatives of the deceased—no matter how far away these relatives may be living.
4. In all Hindu marriages, Balais must play music before the processions and during the marriage.
5. Balai women must not wear gold or silver ornaments; they must not wear fancy gowns or jackets.
6. Balai women must attend all cases of confinement of Hindu women.[12]
7. Balais must render services without demanding remuneration, and must accept whatever a Hindu is pleased to give.
8. If the Balais do not agree to abide by these terms, they must clear out of the villages.

2.10

The Balais refused to comply; and the Hindu element proceeded against them. Balais were not allowed to get water from the village wells; they were not allowed to let their cattle graze. Balais were prohibited from passing through land owned by a Hindu, so that if the field of a Balai was surrounded by fields owned by Hindus, the Balai could have no access to his own field. The Hindus also let their cattle graze down the fields of Balais. The Balais submitted petitions to the Darbar[13] against these persecutions; but as they could get no timely relief, and the oppression continued, hundreds of Balais with their wives and children were obliged to abandon their homes —in which their ancestors had lived for generations—and to migrate to adjoining states: that is, to villages in Dhar, Dewas, Bagli, Bhopal, Gwalior and other states. What happened to them in their new homes may for the present be left out of our consideration.

2.11

The incident at Kavitha[14] in Gujarat happened only last year. The Hindus of Kavitha ordered the Untouchables not to insist upon sending their children to the common village school maintained by the government. What sufferings the Untouchables of Kavitha had to undergo, for daring to exercise a civic right against the wishes of the Hindus, is too well known to need detailed description. Another instance occurred in the village of Zanu, in the Ahmedabad district of Gujarat. In November 1935 some Untouchable women of well-to-do families started fetching water in metal pots. The Hindus looked upon the use of metal pots by Untouchables as an affront to their dignity, and assaulted the Untouchable women for their impudence.

2.12

A most recent event is reported from the village of Chakwara in Jaipur state. It seems from the reports that have appeared in the newspapers that an Untouchable of Chakwara who had returned from a pilgrimage had arranged to give a dinner to his fellow Untouchables of the village, as an act of religious piety. The host desired to treat the guests to a sumptuous meal, and the items served included ghee (butter) also. But while the assembly of Untouchables was engaged in partaking of the food, the Hindus in their hundreds, armed with lathis, rushed to the scene, despoiled the food, and belaboured the Untouchables who left the food, and ran[15] for their lives. And why was this murderous assault committed on defenceless Untouchables? The reason given is that the Untouchable host was impudent enough to serve ghee, and his Untouchable guests were foolish enough to taste it. Ghee is undoubtedly a luxury for the rich. But no one would think that consumption of ghee was a mark of high social status. The Hindus of Chakwara thought otherwise, and in righteous indignation avenged themselves for the wrong done to them by the Untouchables, who insulted them by treating ghee as an item of their food—which they ought to have known could not be theirs—consistently with the dignity of the Hindus. This means that an Untouchable must not use ghee, even if he can afford to buy it, since it is an act of arrogance towards the Hindus. This happened on or about the 1st of April 1936![16]

2.13

Having stated the facts let me now state the case for social reform. In doing this, I will follow Mr Bonnerjee as nearly as I can, and ask the political minded Hindus, "Are you fit for political power even though you do not allow a large class of your own countrymen like the Untouchables to use public schools? Are you fit for political power even though you do not allow them the use of public wells? Are you fit for political power even though you do not allow them the use of public streets? Are you fit for political power even though you do not allow them to wear what apparel or ornaments they like? Are you fit for political power even though you do not allow them to eat any food they like?" I can ask a string of such questions. But these will suffice.

2.14

I wonder what would have been the reply of Mr Bonnerjee. I am sure no sensible man will have the courage to give an affirmative answer. Every Congressman who repeats the dogma of Mill[17] that one country is not fit to rule another country, must admit that one class is not fit to rule another class. How is it then that the 'social reform party' lost the battle? To understand this correctly it is necessary to take note of the kind of social reform which the reformers were agitating for. In this connection it is necessary to make a distinction between social reform in the sense of the reform of the Hindu family, and social reform in the sense of the reorganisation and reconstruction of Hindu society. The former has a relation to widow remarriage, child marriage, etc., while the latter relates to the abolition of the caste system.

2.15

The Social Conference was a body which mainly concerned itself with the reform of the high- caste[18] Hindu family. It consisted mostly of enlightened high-caste Hindus who did not feel the necessity for agitating for the abolition of caste, or had not the courage to agitate for it. They felt quite naturally a greater urge to remove such evils as enforced widowhood, child marriages, etc. —evils which prevailed among them and which were personally felt by them. They did not stand up for the reform of Hindu society. The battle that was fought centred round the question of the reform of the family. It did not relate to social reform in the sense of the break-up of the caste system. It was never put in issue by the reformers. That is the reason why the 'social reform party' lost.

2.16

I am aware that this argument cannot alter the fact that political reform did in fact gain precedence over social reform. But the argument has this much value, if not more: it explains why social reformers lost the battle. It also helps us to understand how limited was the victory which the 'political reform party' obtained over the 'social reform party', and to understand that the view that social reform need not precede political reform is a view which may stand only when by social reform is meant the reform of the family. That political reform cannot with impunity take precedence over social reform in the sense of the reconstruction of society, is a thesis which I am sure cannot be controverted.

2.17

That the makers of political constitutions must take account of social forces is a fact which is recognised by no less a person than Ferdinand Lassalle,[19] the friend and co-worker of Karl Marx.

In addressing a Prussian audience in 1862, Lassalle said:

The constitutional questions are in the first instance not questions of right but questions of might. The actual constitution of a country has its existence only in the actual condition of force which exists in the country: hence political constitutions have value and permanence only when they accurately express those conditions of forces which exist in practice within a society.[20]

2.18

But it is not necessary to go to Prussia.[21] There is evidence at home. What is the significance of the Communal Award,[22] with its allocation of political power in defined proportions to diverse classes and communities? In my view, its significance lies in this: that political constitution must take note of social organisation. It shows that the politicians who denied that the social problem in India had any bearing on the political problem were forced to reckon with the social problem in devising the constitution. The Communal Award is, so to say, the nemesis following upon the indifference to and neglect of social reform. It is a victory for the 'social reform party', which shows that, though defeated, they were in the right in insisting upon the importance of social reform. Many, I know, will not accept this finding. The view is current—and it is pleasant to believe in it—that the Communal Award is unnatural and that it is the result of an unholy alliance between the minorities and the bureaucracv.[23] I do not wish to rely on the Communal Award as a piece of evidence to support my contention, if it is said that it is not good evidence.

2.19

Let us turn to Ireland. What does the history of Irish Home Rule show? It is well known that in the course of the negotiations between the representatives of Ulster and Southern Ireland, Mr Redmond, the representative of Southern Ireland, in order to bring Ulster into a Home Rule constitution common to the whole of Ireland, said to the representatives of Ulster: "Ask any political safeguards you like and you shall have them." What was the reply that Ulstermen gave? Their reply was, "Damn your safeguards, we don't want to be ruled by you on any terms."[24] People who blame the minorities in India ought to consider what would have happened to the political aspirations of the majority, if the minorities had taken the attitude which Ulster took. Judged by the attitude of Ulster to Irish Home Rule, is it nothing that the minorities agreed to be ruled by the majority (which has not shown much sense of statesmanship), provided some safeguards were devised for them? But this is only incidental. The main question is, why did Ulster take this attitude? The only answer I can give is that there was a social problem between Ulster and Southern Ireland: the problem between Catholics and Protestants, which is essentially a problem of caste. That Home Rule in Ireland would be Rome Rule was the way in which the Ulstermen had framed their answer. But that is only another way of stating that it was the social problem of caste between the Catholics and Protestants, which prevented the solution of the political problem. This evidence again is sure to be challenged. It will be urged that here too the hand of the Imperialist was at work.

2.20

But my resources are not exhausted. I will give evidence from the history of Rome. Here no one can say that any evil genius was at work. Anyone who has studied the history of Rome will know that the republican constitution of Rome bore marks having strong resemblance to the Communal Award. When the kingship in Rome was abolished, the kingly power or the Imperium was divided between the consuls and the Pontifex Maximus.[25] In the consuls was vested the secular authority of the king, while the latter took over the religious authority of the king. This republican constitution had provided that of the two consuls, one was to be patrician and the other plebeian.[26] The same constitution had also provided that of the priests under the Pontifex Maximus half were to be plebeians and the other half patricians. Why is it that the republican constitution of Rome had these provisions—which, as I said, resemble so strongly the provisions of the Communal Award? The only answer one can get is that the constitution of republican Rome had to take account of the social division between the patricians and the plebeians, who formed two distinct castes.[27] To sum up, let political reformers turn in any direction they like, they will find that in the making of a constitution, they cannot ignore the problem arising out of the prevailing social order.

2.21

The illustrations which I have taken in support of the proposition that social and religious problems have a bearing on political constitutions seem to be too particular. Perhaps they are. But it should not be supposed that the bearing of the one on the other is limited. On the other hand, one can say that generally speaking, history bears out the proposition that political revolutions have always been preceded by social and religious revolutions. The religious reformation started by Luther[28] was the precursor of the political emancipation of the European people. In England, Puritanism led to the establishment of political liberty. Puritanism founded the new world. It was Puritanism which won the war of American independence, and Puritanism was a religious movement.[29]

2.22

The same is true of the Muslim empire. Before the Arabs became a political power, they had undergone a thorough religious revolution started by the Prophet Muhammad.[30] Even Indian history supports the same conclusion. The political revolution led by Chandragupta was preceded by the religious and social revolution of Buddha.[31] The political revolution led by Shivaji was preceded by the religious and social reform brought about by the saints of Maharashtra.[32] The political revolution of the Sikhs was preceded by the religious and social revolution led by Guru Nanak.[33] It is unnecessary to add more illustrations. These will suffice to show that the emancipation of the mind and the soul is a necessary preliminary for the political expansion of the people.

3

3.1

Let me now turn to the socialists. Can the socialists ignore the problem arising out of the social order? The socialists of India,[34] following their fellows in Europe, are seeking to apply the economic interpretation of history to the facts of India. They propound that man is an economic creature, that his activities and aspirations are bound by economic facts, that property is the only source of power. They therefore preach that political and social reforms are but gigantic illusions, and that economic reform by equalisation of property must have precedence over every other kind of reform. One may join issue with every one of these premises—on which rests the socialists' case for economic reform as having priority over every other kind of reform. One may contend that the economic motive is not the only motive by which man is actuated. That economic power is the only kind of power, no student of human society can accept.

3.2

That the social status of an individual by itself often becomes a source of power and authority is made clear by the sway which the Mahatmas have held over the common man. Why do millionaires in India obey penniless sadhus and fakirs? Why do millions of paupers in India sell their trifling trinkets which constitute their only wealth, and go to Benares and Mecca? That religion is the source of power is illustrated by the history of India, where the priest holds sway over the common man often greater than that of the magistrate, and where everything, even such things as strikes and elections, so easily takes a religious turn and can so easily be given a religious twist.

3.3

Take the case of the plebeians of Rome as a further illustration of the power of religion over man. It throws great light on this point. The plebeians had fought for a share in the supreme executive under the Roman Republic, and had secured the appointment of a plebeian consul elected by a separate electorate constituted by the Comitia Centuriata,[35] which was an assembly of plebeians. They wanted a consul of their own because they felt that the patrician consuls used to discriminate against the plebeians in carrying on the administration. They had apparently obtained a great gain, because under the republican constitution of Rome one consul had the power of vetoing an act of the other consul.

3.4

But did they in fact gain anything? The answer to this question must be in the negative. The plebeians never could get a plebeian consul who could be said to be a strong man, and who could act independently of the patrician consul. In the ordinary course of things the plebeians should have got a strong plebeian consul, in view of the fact that his election was to be by a separate electorate of plebeians. The question is, why did they fail in getting a strong plebeian to officiate as their consul?

3.5

The answer to this question reveals the dominion which religion exercises over the minds of men. It was an accepted creed of the whole Roman populus that no official could enter upon the duties of his office unless the Oracle of Delphi[36] declared that he was acceptable to the goddess. The priests who were in charge of the temple of the goddess of Delphi were all patricians. Whenever therefore the plebeians elected a consul who was known to be a strong party man and opposed to the patricians—or 'communal', to use the term that is current in India—the Oracle invariably declared that he was not acceptable to the goddess. This is how the plebeians were cheated out of their rights.

3.6

But what is worthy of note is that the plebeians permitted themselves to be thus cheated because they too, like the patricians, held firmly the belief that the approval of the goddess was a condition precedent to the taking charge by an official of his duties, and that election by the people was not enough. If the plebeians had contended that election was enough and that the approval by the goddess was not necessary, they would have derived the fullest benefit from the political right which they had obtained. But they did not. They agreed to elect another, less suitable to themselves but more suitable to the goddess—which in fact meant more amenable to the patricians. Rather than give up religion, the plebeians gave up the material gain for which they had fought so hard. Does this not show that religion can be a source of power as great as money, if not greater?

3.7

The fallacy of the socialists[37] lies in supposing that because in the present stage of European society property as a source of power is predominant, the same is true of India, or the same was true of Europe in the past. Religion, social status, and property are all sources of power and authority which one man has to control the liberty of another. One is predominant at one stage; the other is predominant at another stage. That is the only difference. If liberty is the ideal, and if liberty means the destruction of the dominion which one man holds over another, then obviously it cannot be insisted upon that economic reform must be the one kind of reform worthy of pursuit. If the source of power and dominion is, at any given time or in any given society, social and religious, then social reform and religious reform must be accepted as the necessary sort of reform.

3.8

One can thus attack the doctrine of economic interpretation of history adopted by the socialists of India. But I recognise that the economic interpretation of history is not necessary for the validity of the socialist contention that equalisation of property is the only real reform and that it must precede everything else. However, what I would like to ask the socialists is this: Can you have economic reform without first bringing about a reform of the social order? The socialists of India do not seem to have considered this question.[38] I do not wish to do them an injustice. I give below a quotation from a letter which a prominent socialist wrote a few days ago to a friend of mine, in which he said, "I do not believe that we can build up a free society in India so long as there is a trace of this ill- treatment and suppression of one class by another. Believing as I do in a socialist ideal, inevitably I believe in perfect equality in the treatment of various classes and groups. I think that socialism offers the only true remedy for this as well as other problems."

3.9

Now the question that I would like to ask is: Is it enough for a socialist to say, "I believe in perfect equality in the treatment of the various classes?" To say that such a belief is enough is to disclose a complete lack of understanding of what is involved in socialism. If socialism is a practical programme and is not merely an ideal, distant and far off, the question for a socialist is not whether he believes in equality. The question for him is whether he minds one class ill- treating and suppressing another class as a matter of system, as a matter of principle— and thus allow tyranny and oppression to continue to divide one class from another.

3.10

Let me analyse the factors that are involved in the realisation of socialism, in order to explain fully my point. Now it is obvious that the economic reform contemplated by the socialists cannot come about unless there is a revolution resulting in the seizure of power. That seizure of power must be by a proletariat. The first question I ask is: Will the proletariat of India combine to bring about this revolution? What will move men to such an action? It seems to me that, other things being equal, the only thing that will move one man to take such an action is the feeling that other men with whom he is acting are actuated by feelings of equality and fraternity and—above all—of justice. Men will not join in a revolution for the equalisation of property unless they know that after the revolution is achieved they will be treated equally, and that there will be no discrimination of caste and creed.

3.11

The assurance of a socialist leading the revolution that he does not believe in caste, I am sure, will not suffice. The assurance must be the assurance proceeding from a much deeper foundation —namely, the mental attitude of the compatriots towards one another in their spirit of personal equality and fraternity. Can it be said that the proletariat of India, poor as it is, recognises no distinctions except that of the rich and the poor? Can it be said that the poor in India recognise no such distinctions of caste or creed, high or low? If the fact is that they do, what unity of front can be expected from such a proletariat in its action against the rich? How can there be a revolution if the proletariat cannot present a united front?

3.12

Suppose for the sake of argument that by some freak of fortune a revolution does take place and the socialists come into power, will they not have to deal with the problems created by the particular social order prevalent in India? I can't see how a socialist state in India can function for a second without having to grapple with the problems created by the prejudices which make Indian people observe the distinctions of high and low, clean and unclean. If socialists are not to be content with the mouthing of fine phrases, if the socialists wish to make socialism a definite reality, then they must recognise that the problem of social reform is fundamental, and that for them there is no escape from it.

3.13

That the social order prevalent in India is a matter which a socialist must deal with; that unless he does so he cannot achieve his revolution; and that if he does achieve it as a result of good fortune, he will have to grapple with the social order if he wishes to realise his ideal—is a proposition which in my opinion is incontrovertible. He will be compelled to take account of caste after the revolution, if he does not take account of it before the revolution. This is only another way of saying that, turn in any direction you like, caste is the monster that crosses your path. You cannot have political reform, you cannot have economic reform, unless you kill this monster.

4

4.1

It is a pity that caste even today has its defenders. The defences are many. It is defended on the ground that the caste system is but another name for division of labour; and if division of labour is a necessary feature of every civilised society, then it is argued that there is nothing wrong in the caste system. Now the first thing that is to be urged against this view is that the caste system is not merely a division of labour. It is also a division of labourers.[39] Civilised society undoubtedly needs division of labour. But in no civilised society is division of labour accompanied by this unnatural division of labourers into watertight compartments. The caste system is not merely a division of labourers—which is quite different from division of labour—it is a hierarchy in which the divisions of labourers are graded one above the other. In no other country is the division of labour accompanied by this gradation of labourers.

4.2

There is also a third point of criticism against this view of the caste system. This division of labour is not spontaneous; it is not based on natural aptitudes. Social and individual efficiency requires us to develop the capacity of an individual to the point of competency to choose and to make his own career. This principle is violated in the caste system, in so far as it involves an attempt to appoint tasks to individuals in advance—selected not on the basis of trained original capacities, but on that of the social status of the parents.

4.3

Looked at from another point of view, this stratification of occupations which is the result of the caste system is positively pernicious. Industry is never static.[41] It undergoes rapid and abrupt changes. With such changes, an individual must be free to change his occupation. Without such freedom to adjust himself to changing circumstances, it would be impossible for him to gain his livelihood. Now the caste system will not allow Hindus to take to occupations where they are wanted, if they do not belong to the by heredity. If a Hindu is seen to starve rather than take to new occupations not assigned to his caste, the reason is to be found in the caste system. By not permitting readjustment of occupations, caste becomes a direct cause of much of the unemployment we see in the country.

4.4

As a form of division of labour, the caste system suffers from another serious defect. The division of labour brought about by the caste system is not a division based on choice. Individual sentiment, individual preference, has no place in it. It is based on the dogma of predestination. Considerations of social efficiency would compel us to recognise that the greatest evil in the industrial system is not so much poverty and the suffering that it involves, as the fact that so many persons have callings which make no appeal to those who are engaged in them. Such callings constantly provoke one to aversion, ill will and the desire to evade.[42]

4.5

There are many occupations in India which, on account of the fact that they are regarded as degraded by the Hindus, provoke those who are engaged in them to aversion. There is a constant desire to evade and escape from such occupations, which arises solely because of the blighting effect which they produce upon those who follow them, owing to the slight and stigma cast upon them by the Hindu religion. What efficiency can there be in a system under which neither men's hearts nor their minds are in their work? As an economic organisation caste is therefore a harmful institution, inasmuch as it involves the subordination of man's natural powers and inclinations to the exigencies of social rules.

5

5.1

Some have dug a biological trench in defence of the caste system. It is said that the object of caste was to preserve purity of race and purity of blood. Now ethnologists[43] are of the opinion that men of pure race exist nowhere and that there has been a mixture of all races in all parts of the world. Especially is this the case with the people of India. Mr D.R. Bhandarkar in his paper on "Foreign Elements in the Hindu Population" has stated that "There is hardly a class or caste in India which has not a foreign strain in it. There is an admixture of alien blood not only among the warrior classes—the Rajputs and the Marathas—but also among the Brahmins who are under the happy delusion that they are free from all foreign elements."[44] The caste system cannot be said to have grown as a means of preventing the admixture of races, or as a means of maintaining purity of blood.

5.2

As a matter of fact the caste system came into being long after the different races of India had commingled in blood and culture.[45] To hold that distinctions of castes are really distinctions of race, and to treat different castes as though they were so many different races, is a gross perversion of facts. What racial affinity is there between the Brahmin of the Punjab and the Brahmin of Madras? What racial affinity is there between the Untouchable of Bengal and the Untouchable of Madras? What racial difference is there between the Brahmin of the Punjab and the Chamar of the Punjab? What racial difference is there between the Brahmin of Madras and the Pariah of Madras? The Brahmin of the Punjab is racially of the same stock as the Chamar of the Punjab, and the Brahmin of Madras is of the same race as the Pariah of Madras.

5.3

The caste system does not demarcate racial division. The caste system is a social division of people of the same race. Assuming it, however, to be a case of racial divisions, one may ask: What harm could there be if a mixture of races and of blood was permitted to take place in India by intermarriages between different castes? Men are no doubt divided from animals by so deep a distinction that science recognises men and animals as two distinct species. But even scientists who believe in purity of races do not assert that the different races constitute different species of men. They are only varieties of one and the same species. As such they can interbreed and produce an offspring which is capable of breeding and which is not sterile.

5.4

An immense lot of nonsense is talked about heredity and eugenics[46] in defence of the caste system. Few would object to the caste system if it was in accord with the basic principle of eugenics, because few can object to the improvement of the race by judicious mating. But one fails to understand how the caste system secures judicious mating. The caste system is a negative thing. It merely prohibits persons belonging to different castes from intermarrying. It is not a positive method of selecting which two among a given caste should marry.

5.5

If caste is eugenic in origin, then the origin of sub-castes must also be eugenic. But can anyone seriously maintain that the origin of sub-castes is eugenic? I think it would be absurd to contend for such a proposition, and for a very obvious reason. If caste means race, then differences of subcastes cannot mean differences of race, because sub-castes become ex hypothesi sub-divisions of one and the same race. Consequently the bar against intermarrying and inter-dining between sub- castes cannot be for the purpose of maintaining purity of race or of blood. If sub-castes cannot be eugenic in origin, there cannot be any substance in the contention that caste is eugenic in origin.

5.6

Again, if caste is eugenic in origin[47] one can understand the bar against intermarriage. But what is the purpose of the interdict placed on inter-dining between castes and sub-castes alike? Inter- dining cannot infect blood, and therefore cannot be the cause either of the improvement or of the deterioration of the race.

5.7

This shows that caste has no scientific origin, and that those who are attempting to give it a eugenic basis are trying to support by science what is grossly unscientific. Even today, eugenics cannot become a practical possibility unless we have definite knowledge regarding the laws of heredity. Prof Bateson in his Mendel's Principles of Heredity says, "There is nothing in the descent of the higher mental qualities to suggest that they follow any single system of transmission. It is likely that both they and the more marked developments of physical powers result rather from the coincidence of numerous factors than from the possession of any one genetic element."[48] To argue that the caste system was eugenic in its conception is to attribute to the forefathers of present-day Hindus a knowledge of heredity which even the modern scientists do not possess.

5.8

A tree should be judged by the fruits it yields. If caste is eugenic, what sort of a race of men should it have produced? Physically speaking the Hindus are a C3 people.[49] They are a race of pygmies and dwarfs, stunted in stature and wanting in stamina. It is a nation nine-tenths of which is declared to be unfit for military service. This shows that the caste system does not embody the eugenics of modern scientists. It is a social system which embodies the arrogance and selfishness of a perverse section of the Hindus who were superior enough in social status to set it in fashion, and who had the authority to force it on their inferiors.

6

6.1

Caste does not result in economic efficiency. Caste cannot improve, and has not improved, race.[50] Caste has, however, done one thing. It has completely disorganised and demoralised the Hindus.

6.2

The first and foremost thing that must be recognised is that Hindu society is a myth. The name Hindu is itself a foreign name.[51] It was given by the Mahomedans to the natives for the purpose of distinguishing themselves. It does not occur in any Sanskrit work prior to the Mahomedan invasion. They did not feel the necessity of a common name, because they had no conception of their having constituted a community. Hindu society as such does not exist. It is only a collection of castes. Each caste is conscious of its existence. Its survival is the be-all and end-all of its existence. Castes do not even form a federation. A caste has no feeling that it is affiliated to other castes, except when there is a Hindu—Moslem riot. On all other occasions each caste endeavours to segregate itself and to distinguish itself from other castes.

6.3

Each caste not only dines among itself and marries among itself, but each caste prescribes its own distinctive dress. What other explanation can there be of the innumerable styles of dress worn by the men and women of India, which so amuse the tourists? Indeed the ideal Hindu must be like a rat living in his own hole, refusing to have any contact with others. There is an utter lack among the Hindus of what the sociologists call 'consciousness of kind'.[52] There is no Hindu consciousness of kind. In every Hindu the consciousness that exists is the consciousness of his caste. That is the reason why the Hindus cannot be said to form a society or a nation.

6.4

There are, however, many Indians whose patriotism does not permit them to admit that Indians are not a nation, that they are only an amorphous mass of people. They have insisted that underlying the apparent diversity there is a fundamental unity which marks the life of the Hindus, inasmuch as there is a similarity of those habits and customs, beliefs and thoughts, which obtain all over the continent of India. Similarity in habits and customs, beliefs and thoughts, there is. But one cannot accept the conclusion that therefore, the Hindus constitute a society. To do so is to misunderstand the essentials which go to make up a society. Men do not become a society by living in physical proximity, any more than a man ceases to be a member of his society by living so many miles away from other men.

6.5

Secondly, similarity in habits and customs, beliefs and thoughts, is not enough to constitute men into society. Things may be passed physically from one to another like bricks. In the same wav habits and customs, beliefs and thoughts of one group may be taken over by another group, and there may thus appear a similarity between the two. Culture spreads by diffusion, and that is why one finds similarity between various primitive tribes in the matter of their habits and customs, beliefs and thoughts, although they do not live in proximity. But no one could say that because there was this similarity, the primitive tribes constituted one society. This is because similarity in certain things is not enough to constitute a society.

6.6

Men constitute a society because they have things which they possess in common. To have similar things is totally different from possessing things in common. And the only way by which men can come to possess things in common with one another is by being in communication[53] with one another. This is merely another wav of saving that society continues to exist by communication—- indeed, in communication.[54] To make it concrete, it is not enough if men act in a way which agrees with the acts of others. Parallel activity, even if similar, is not sufficient to bind men into a society.

6.7

This is proved by the fact that the festivals observed by the different castes amongst the Hindus are the same. Yet these parallel performances of similar festivals by the different castes have not bound them into one integral whole. For that purpose what is necessary is for a man to share and participate in a common activity, so that the same emotions are aroused in him that animate the others. Making the individual a sharer or partner in the associated activity, so that he feels its success as his success, its failure as his failure, is the real thing that binds men and makes a society of them. The caste system prevents common activity; and by preventing common activity, it has prevented the Hindus from becoming a society with a unified life and a consciousness of its own being.

7

7.1

The Hindus often complain of the isolation and exclusiveness of a gang or a clique and blame them for antisocial spirit. But they conveniently forget that this anti-social spirit is the worst feature of their own caste system. One caste enjoys singing a hymn of hate against another caste as much as the Germans enjoyed singing their hymn of hate against the English during the last war. The literature of the Hindus is full of caste genealogies in which an attempt is made to give a noble origin to one caste and an ignoble origin to other castes. The Sahyadrikhand is a notorious instance of this class of literature.[55]

7.2

This anti-social spirit is not confined to caste alone. It has gone deeper and has poisoned the mutual relations of the sub-castes as well. In my province the Golak Brahmins, Deorukha Brahmins, Karada Brahmins, Palshe Brahmins,[56] and Chitpavan Brahmins[57] all claim to be sub- divisions of the Brahmin caste. But the anti-social spirit that prevails between them is quite as marked and quite as virulent as the anti-social spirit that prevails between them and other non-Brahmin castes. There is nothing strange in this. An anti-social spirit is found wherever one group has 'interests of its own which shut it out from full interaction with other groups, so that its prevailing purpose is protection of what it has got.

7.3

This anti-social spirit, this spirit of protecting their own interests, is as much a marked feature of the different castes in their isolation from one another as it is of nations in their isolation. The Brahmin's primary concern is to protect 'his interests' against those of the non-Brahmins; and the non-Brahmins' primary concern is to protect their interests against those of the Brahmins. The Hindus, therefore, are not merely an assortment of castes, but are so many warring groups, each living for itself and for its selfish ideal.

7.4

There is another feature of caste which is deplorable. The ancestors of the present-day English fought on one side or the other in the Wars of the Roses and the Cromwellian War.[58] But the descendants of those who fought on the one side do not bear any animosity—any grudge—against the descendants of those who fought on the other side. The feud is forgotten. But the present-day non-Brahmins cannot forgive the present- day Brahmins for the insult their ancestors gave to Shivaji.[59] The present-day Kayasthas will not forgive the present-day Brahmins for the infamy cast upon their forefathers by the forefathers of the latter.[60] To what is this difference due?

Obviously to the caste system. The existence of caste and caste consciousness has served to keep the memory of past feuds between castes green, and has prevented solidarity.

8

8.1

The recent discussion about the excluded and partially excluded[61] areas has served to draw attention to the position of what are called the aboriginal tribes in India.[62] They number about thirteen million, if not more. Apart from the question of whether their exclusion from the new Constitution[63] is proper or improper, the fact still remains that these aborigines have remained in their primitive uncivilised state[64] in a land which boasts of a civilisation thousands of years old. Not only are they not civilised, but some of them follow pursuits which have led to their being classified as criminals.[65]

8.2

Thirteen million people living in the midst of civilisation are still in a savage state, and are leading the life of hereditary criminals! But the Hindus have never felt ashamed of it. This is a phenomenon which in my view is quite unparalleled. What is the cause of this shameful state of affairs? Why has no attempt been made to civilise these aborigines and to lead them to take to a more honourable way of making a living?

8.3

The Hindus will probably seek to account for this savage state of the aborigines by attributing to them congenital stupidity. They will probably not admit that the aborigines have remained savages because they had made no effort to civilise them, to give them medical aid, to reform them, to make them good citizens. But supposing a Hindu wished to do what the Christian missionary is doing for these aborigines, could he have done it? I submit not. Civilising the aborigines means adopting them as your own, living in their midst, and cultivating fellow-feeling—in short, loving them. How is it possible for a Hindu to do this? His whole life is one anxious effort to preserve his caste. Caste is his precious possession which he must save at any cost. He cannot consent to lose it by establishing contact with the aborigines, the remnants of the hateful anaryas[66] of the Vedic days.

8.4

Not that a Hindu could not be taught the sense of duty to fallen humanity, but the trouble is that no amount of sense of duty can enable him to overcome his duty to preserve his caste. Caste is, therefore, the real explanation as to why the Hindu has let the savage remain a savage in the midst of his civilisation without blushing, or without feeling any sense of remorse or repentance. The Hindu has not realised that these aborigines are a source of potential danger. If these savages remain savages, they may not do any harm to the Hindus. But if they are reclaimed by non-Hindus and converted to their faiths, they will swell the ranks of the enemies of the Hindus. If this happens, the Hindu will have to thank himself and his caste system.

9

9.1

Not only has the Hindu made no effort for the humanitarian cause of civilising the savages, but the higher-caste Hindus have deliberately prevented the lower castes who are within the pale of Hinduism from rising to the cultural level of the higher castes. I will give two instances, one of the Sonars and the other of the Pathare Prabhus.[67] Both are communities quite well known in Maharashtra. Like the rest of the communities desiring to raise their status, these two communities were at one time endeavouring to adopt some of the ways and habits of the Brahmins.

9.2

The Sonars were styling themselves Daivadnya Brahmins[68] and were wearing their dhotis with folds in them, and using the word 'namaskar' for salutation. Both the folded way of wearing the dhoti and the namaskar were special to the Brahmins. The Brahmins did not like this imitation and this attempt by Sonars to pass off as Brahmins. Under the authority of the Peshwas, the Brahmins successfully put down this attempt on the part of the Sonars to adopt the ways of the Brahmins. They even got the president of the councils of the East India Company's settlement in Bombay to issue a prohibitory order against the Sonars residing in Bombay.

9.3

At one time the Pathare Prabhus had widow remarriage as a custom of their caste. This custom of widow remarriage was later on looked upon as a mark of social inferiority by some members of the caste, especially because it was contrary to the custom prevalent among the Brahmins. With the object of raising the status of their community, some Pathare Prabhus sought to stop this practice of widow remarriage that was prevalent in their caste. The community was divided into two camps, one for and the other against the innovation. The Peshwas took the side of those in favour of widow remarriage, and thus virtually prohibited the Pathare Prabhus from following the ways of the Brahmins.

9.4

The Hindus criticise the Mahomedans for having spread their religion by the use of the sword. They also ridicule Christianity on the score of the Inquisition.[69] But really speaking, who is better and more worthy of our respect—the Mahomedans and Christians who attempted to thrust down the throats of unwilling persons what they regarded as necessary for their salvation, or the Hindu who would not spread the light, who would endeavour to keep others in darkness, who would not consent to share his intellectual and social inheritance with those who are ready and willing to make it a part of their own make-up? I have no hesitation in saying that if the Mahomedan has been cruel, the Hindu has been mean; and meanness is worse than cruelty.

10

10.1

Whether the Hindu religion was or was not a missionary religion has been a controversial issue.[70] Some hold the view that it was never a missionary religion. Others hold that it was. That the Hindu religion was once a missionary religion must be admitted. It could not have spread over the face of India, if it was not a missionary religion. That today it is not a missionary religion is also a fact which must be accepted. The question therefore is not whether or not the Hindu religion was a missionary religion. The real question is, why did the Hindu religion cease to be a missionary religion?[71]

10.2

My answer is this: the Hindu religion ceased to be a missionary religion when the caste system grew up among the Hindus. Caste is inconsistent with conversion. Inculcation of beliefs and dogmas is not the only problem that is involved in conversion. To find a place for the convert in the social life of the community is another, and a much more important, problem that arises in connection with conversion. That problem is where to place the convert, in what caste? It is a problem which must baffle every Hindu wishing to make aliens convert to his religion.

10.3

Unlike a club, the membership of a caste is not open to all and sundry.[72] The law of caste confines its membership to persons born in the caste. Castes are autonomous, and there is no authority anywhere to compel a caste to admit a newcomer to its social life. Hindu society being a collection of castes, and each caste being a closed corporation, there is no place for a convert. Thus it is caste which has prevented the Hindus from expanding and from absorbing other religious communities. So long as caste remains, Hindu religion cannot be made a missionary religion, and shuddhi[73] will be both a folly and a futility.

11

11.1

The reasons which have made shuddhi impossible for Hindus are also responsible for making sangathan[74] impossible. The idea underlying sangathan is to remove from the mind of the Hindu that timidity and cowardice which so painfully mark him off from the Mahomedan and the Sikh, and which have led him to adopt the low ways of treachery and cunning for protecting himself. The question naturally arises: From where does the Sikh or the Mahomedan derive his strength, which makes him brave and fearless? I am sure it is not due to relative superiority of physical strength, diet or drill. It is due to the strength arising out of the feeling that all Sikhs will come to the rescue of a Sikh when he is in danger, and that all Mahomedans will rush to save a Muslim if he is attacked.

11.2

The Hindu can derive no such strength. He cannot feel assured that his fellows will come to his help. Being one and fated to be alone, he remains powerless, develops timidity and cowardice, and in a fight surrenders or runs away. The Sikh as well as the Muslim stands fearless and gives battle, because he knows that though one he will not be alone. The presence of this belief in the one helps him to hold out, and the absence of it in the other makes him to give way.

11.3

If you pursue this matter further and ask what is it that enables the Sikh and the Mahomedan to feel so assured, and why is the Hindu filled with such despair in the matter of help and assistance, you will find that the reasons for this difference lie in the difference in their associated mode of living.[75] The associated mode of life practised by the Sikhs and the Mahomedans produces fellow-feeling. The associated mode of life of the Hindus does not. Among Sikhs and Muslims there is a social cement which makes them bhais.[76] Among Hindus there is no such cement, and one Hindu does not regard another Hindu as his bhai. This explains why a Sikh says and feels that one Sikh, or one Khalsa, is equal to sava lakh men.[77] This explains why one Mahomedan is equal to a crowd of Hindus. This difference is undoubtedly a difference due to caste. So long as caste remains, there will be no sangathan; and so long as there is no sangathan the Hindu will remain weak and meek.

11.4

The Hindus claim to be a very tolerant people. In my opinion this is a mistake. On many occasions they can be intolerant, and if on some occasions they are tolerant, that is because they are too weak to oppose or too indifferent to oppose. This indifference of the Hindus has become so much a part of their nature that a Hindu will quite meekly tolerate an insult as well as a wrong. You see amongst them, to use the words of Morris, "The great treacling down the little, the strong beating down the weak, cruel men fearing not, kind men daring not and wise men caring not."[78] With the Hindu gods all-forbearing, it is not difficult to imagine the pitiable condition of the wronged and the oppressed among the Hindus. Indifferentism is the worst kind of disease that can infect a people. Why is the Hindu so indifferent? In my opinion this indifferentism is the result of the caste system, which has made sangathan and cooperation even for a good cause impossible.

12

12.1

The assertion by the individual of his own opinions and beliefs, his own independence and interest—over and against group standards, group authority, and group interests— is the beginning of all reform. But whether the reform will continue depends upon what scope the group affords for such individual assertion. If the group is tolerant and fair-minded in dealing with such individuals, they will continue to assert, and in the end will succeed in converting their fellows. On the other hand if the group is intolerant, and does not bother about the means it adopts to stifle such individuals, they will perish and the reform will die out.

12.2

Now a caste has an unquestioned right to excommunicate any man who is guilty of breaking the rules of the caste; and when it is realised that excommunication involves a complete cesser of social intercourse, it will be agreed that as a form of punishment there is really little to choose between excommunication and death. No wonder individual Hindus have not had the courage to assert their independence by breaking the barriers of caste.

12.3

It is true that man cannot get on with his fellows. But it is also true that he cannot do without them. He would like to have the society of his fellows on his terms. If he cannot get it on his terms, then he will be ready to have it on any terms, even amounting to complete surrender. This is because he cannot do without society. A caste is ever ready to take advantage of the helplessness of a man, and to insist upon complete conformity to its code in letter and in spirit.

12.4

A caste can easily organise itself into a conspiracy to make the life of a reformer hell; and if a conspiracy is a crime, I do not understand why such a nefarious act as an attempt to excommunicate a person for daring to act contrary to the rules of caste should not be made an offence punishable by law. But as it is, even law gives each caste autonomy to regulate its membership and punish dissenters with excommunication. Caste in the hands of the orthodox has been a powerful weapon for persecuting the reformers and for killing all reform.

13

13.1

The effect of caste on the ethics of the Hindus is simply deplorable. Caste has killed public spirit. Caste has destroyed the sense of public charity. Caste has made public opinion impossible. A Hindu's public is his caste. His responsibility is only to his caste. His loyalty is restricted only to his caste. Virtue has become caste-ridden, and morality has become caste-bound. There is no sympathy for the deserving. There is no appreciation of the meritorious. There is no charity to the needy. Suffering as such calls for no response. There is charity, but it begins with caste and ends with caste. There is sympathy, but not for men of other castes.

13.2

Would a Hindu acknowledge and follow the leadership of a great and good man? The case of a Mahatma apart, the answer must be that he will follow a leader if he is a man of his caste. A Brahmin will follow a leader only if he is a Brahmin, a Kayastha if he is a Kayastha, and so on. The capacity to appreciate merits in a man, apart from his caste, does not exist in a Hindu. There is appreciation of virtue, but only when the man is a fellow caste-man. The whole morality is as bad as tribal morality. My caste-man, right or wrong; my casteman, good or bad. It is not a case of standing by virtue or not standing by vice. It is a case of standing by, or not standing by, caste. Have not Hindus committed treason against their country in the interests of their castes?

14

14.1

I would not be surprised if some of you have grown weary listening to this tiresome tale of the sad effects which caste has produced. There is nothing new in it. I will therefore turn to the constructive side of the problem. What is your ideal society if you do not want caste, is a question that is bound to be asked of you. If you ask me, my ideal would be a society based on liberty, equality, and fraternity. And why not?

14.2

What objection can there be to fraternity? I cannot imagine any. An ideal society should be mobile, should be full of channels for conveying a change taking place in one part to other parts. In an ideal society there should be many interests consciously communicated and shared. There should be varied and free points of contact with other modes of association. In other words there must be social endosmosis.[79] This is fraternity, which is only another name for democracy. Democracy is not merely a form of government. It is primarily a mode of associated living, of conjoint communicated experience.[80] It is essentially an attitude of respect and reverence towards fellow men.

14.3

Any objection to liberty? Few object to liberty in the sense of a right to free movement, in the sense of a right to life and limb. There is no objection to liberty in the sense of a right to property, tools and materials, as being necessary for earning a living, to keep the body in a due state of health. Why not allow a person the liberty to benefit from an effective and competent use of a person's powers? The supporters of caste who would allow liberty in the sense of a right to life, limb, and property, would not readily consent to liberty in this sense, inasmuch as it involves liberty to choose one's profession.

14.4

But to object to this kind of liberty is to perpetuate slavery. For slavery does not merely mean a legalised form of subjection. It means a state of society in which some men are forced to accept from others the purposes which control their conduct. This condition obtains even where there is no slavery in the legal sense. It is found where, as in the caste system, some persons are compelled to carry on certain prescribed callings which are not of their choice.

14.5

Any objection to equality? This has obviously been the most contentious part of the slogan of the French Revolution. The objections to equality may be sound, and one may have to admit that all men are not equal. But what of that? Equality may be a fiction, but nonetheless one must accept it as the governing principle. A man's power is dependent upon (1) physical heredity; (2) social inheritance or endowment in the form of parental care, education, accumulation of scientific knowledge, everything which enables him to be more efficient than the savage; and finally, (3) on his own efforts. In all these three respects men are undoubtedly unequal. But the question is, shall we treat them as unequal because they are unequal? This is a question which the opponents of equality must answer.

14.6

From the standpoint of the individualist, it may be just to treat men unequally so far as their efforts are unequal. It may be desirable to give as much incentive as possible to the full development of everyone's powers. But what would happen if men were treated as unequally as they are unequal in the first two respects?[81] It is obvious that those individuals also in whose favour there is birth, education, family name, business connections, and inherited wealth, would be selected in the race. But selection under such circumstances would not be a selection of the able. It would be the selection of the privileged. The reason, therefore, which forces that in the third respect we should treat men unequally, demands that in the first two respects we should treat men as equally as possible.

14.7

On the other hand, it can be urged that if it is good for the social body to get the most out of its members, it can get the most out of them only by making them equal as far as possible at the very start of the race. That is one reason why we cannot escape equality. But there is another reason why we must accept equality. A statesman is concerned with vast numbers of people. He has neither the time nor the knowledge to draw fine distinctions and to treat each one equitably, i.e., according to need or according to capacity. However desirable or reasonable an equitable treatment of men may be, humanity is not capable of assortment and classification. The statesman, therefore, must follow some rough and ready rule, and that rough and ready rule is to treat all men alike, not because they are alike but because classification and assortment is impossible. The doctrine of equality is glaringly fallacious but, taking all in all, it is the only way a statesman can proceed in politics—which is a severely practical affair and which demands a severely practical test.

15

15.1

But there is a set of reformers who hold out a different ideal. They go by the name of the Arya Samajists,[82] and their ideal of social organisation is what is called chaturvarnya, or the division of society into four classes instead of the four thousand castes that we have in India. To make it more attractive and to disarm opposition, the protagonists of chaturvarnya take great care to point out that their chaturvarnya is based not on birth but on guna (worth).[83] At the outset, I must confess that notwithstanding the worth-basis of this chaturvarnya, it is an ideal to which I cannot reconcile myself.

15.2

In the first place, if under the chaturvarnya of the Arya Samajists an individual is to take his place in Hindu society according to his worth, I do not understand why the Arya Samajists insist upon labelling men as Brahmin, Kshatriya, Vaishya and Shudra. A learned man would be honoured without his being labelled a Brahmin. A soldier would be respected without his being designated a Kshatriya. If European society honours its soldiers and its servants[84] without giving them permanent labels, why should Hindu society find it difficult to do so, is a question which Arya Samajists have not cared to consider.

15.3

There is another objection to the continuance of these labels. All reform consists in a change in the notions, sentiments and mental attitudes of the people towards men and things.[85] It is common experience that certain names become associated with certain notions and sentiments which determine a person's attitude towards men and things. The names Brahmin, Kshatriya, Vaishya and Shudra are names which are associated with a definite and fixed notion in the mind of every Hindu. That notion is that of a hierarchy based on birth.

15.4

So long as these names continue, Hindus will continue to think of the Brahmin, Kshatriya, Vaishya and Shudra as hierarchical divisions of high and low, based on birth, and to act accordingly. The Hindu must be made to unlearn all this. But how can this happen if the old labels remain and continue to recall to his mind old notions? If new notions are to be inculcated in the minds of people, it is necessary to give them new names. To continue the old names is to make the reform futile. To allow this chaturvarnya based on worth to be designated by such stinking labels as Brahmin, Kshatriya, Vaishya, Shudra, indicative of social divisions based on birth, is a snare.

16

16.1

To me this chaturvarnya with its old labels is utterly repellent, and mv whole being rebels against it. But I do not wish to rest mv objection to chaturvarnya on mere grounds of sentiments. There are more solid grounds on which I rely for my opposition to it. A close examination of this ideal has convinced me that as a system of social organisation, chaturvarnya is impracticable, is harmful, and has turned out to be a miserable failure.[87] From a practical point of view, the system of chaturvarnya raises several difficulties which its protagonists do not seem to have taken into account. The principle underlying caste is fundamentally different from the principle underlying chaturvarnya.[88] Not only are they fundamentally different, but they are also fundamentally opposed.

16.2

The former, chaturvarnya, is based on worth. How are you going to compel people who have acquired a higher status based on birth, without reference to their worth, to vacate that status? How are you going to compel people to recognise the status due to a man, in accordance with his worth, who is occupying a lower status based on his birth? For this, you must first break up the caste system, in order to be able to establish the chaturvarnya system. How are you going to reduce the four thousand castes, based on birth, to the four varnas, based on worth? This is the first difficulty which the protagonists of chaturvarnya must grapple with.

16.3

There is a second difficulty which the protagonists of chaturvarnya must grapple with, if they wish to make the establishment of chaturvarnya a success.[89] Chaturvarnya presupposes that you can classify people into four definite classes. Is this possible?[90] In this respect, the ideal of chaturvarnya has, as you will see, a close affinity to the Platonic ideal. To Plato, men fell by nature into three classes. In some individuals, he believed,[91] mere appetites dominated. He assigned them to the labouring and trading classes. Others revealed to him that over and above appetites, they had a courageous disposition. He classed them as defenders in war and guardians of internal peace. Others showed a capacity to grasp the universal—the reason underlying things. He made them the law-givers of the people.

16.4

The criticism to which Plato's Republic is subject is also the criticism which must apply to the system of chaturvarnya, in so far as it proceeds upon the possibility of an accurate classification of men into four distinct classes.[92] The chief criticism against Plato is that his idea of lumping individuals into a few sharply marked-off classes is a very superficial view of man and his powers. Plato had no perception of the uniqueness of every individual, of his incommensurability with others, of each individual as forming a class of his own. He had no recognition of the infinite diversity of active tendencies, and the combination of tendencies of which an individual is capable. To him, there were types of faculties or powers in the individual constitution.

16.5

All this is demonstrably wrong. Modern science has shown that the lumping together of individuals into a few sharply marked-off classes is a superficial view of man, not worthy of serious consideration. Consequently, the utilisation of the qualities of individuals is incompatible with their stratification by classes, since the qualities of individuals are so variable. Chaturvarnya must fail for the very reason for which Plato's Republic must fail—namely, that it is not possible to pigeon men into holes according to class.[93] That it is impossible to accurately classify people into four definite classes is proved by the fact that the original four classes have now become four thousand castes.

16.6

There is a third difficulty in the way of the establishment of the system of chaturvarnya. How are you going to maintain the system of chaturvarnya, supposing it was established? One[94] important requirement for the successful working of chaturvarnya is the maintenance[95] of the penal system which could maintain it by its sanction. The system of chaturvarnya must perpetually face the problem of the transgressor. Unless there is a penalty attached to the act of transgression, men will not keep to their respective classes. The whole system will break down, being contrary to human nature. Chaturvarnya cannot subsist by its own inherent goodness. It must be enforced by law.

16.7

That without penal sanction the ideal of chaturvarnya cannot be realised is proved by the story in the Ramayana of Rama killing Shambuka.[96] Some people seem to blame Rama because he wantonly and without reason killed Shambuka. But to blame Rama for killing Shambuka is to misunderstand the whole situation. Ram Raj was a raj based on chaturvarnya. As a king, Rama was bound to maintain chaturvarnya. It was his duty therefore to kill Shambuka, the Shudra who had transgressed his class and wanted to be a Brahmin. This is the reasonwhy Rama killed Shambuka. But this also shows that penal sanction is necessary for the maintenance of chaturvarnya. Not only penal sanction is necessary, but the penalty of death is necessary. That is why Rama did not inflict on Shambuka a lesser punishment. That is why the Manusmriti[97] prescribes such heavy sentences as cutting off the tongue, or pouring of molten lead in the ears, of the Shudra who recites or hears the Veda.[98] The supporters of chaturvarnya must give an assurance that they could successfully classify men, and that they could induce modern society in the twentieth century to re-forge the penal sanctions of the Manusmriti.

16.8

The protagonists of chaturvarnya do not seem to have considered what is to happen to women in their system. Are they also to be divided into four classes, Brahmin, Kshatriya, Vaishya and Shudra? Or are they to be allowed to take the status of their husbands? If the status of the woman is to be the consequence of marriage, what becomes of the underlying principle of chaturvarnya— namely, that the status of a person should be based upon the worth of that person? If they are to be classified according to their worth, is their classification to be nominal or real?

16.9

If it is to be nominal, then it is useless; and then the protagonists of chaturvarnya must admit that their system does not apply to women. If it is real, are the protagonists of chaturvarnya prepared to follow the logical consequences of applying it to women? They must be prepared to have women priests and women soldiers. Hindu society has grown accustomed to women teachers and women barristers. It may grow accustomed to women brewers and women butchers. But he would be a bold person who would say that it will allow women priests and women soldiers. But that will be the logical outcome of applying chaturvarnya to women. Given these difficulties, I think no one except a congenital idiot could hope for and believe in a successful regeneration of chaturvarnya.

17

17.1

Assuming that chaturvarnya is practicable, I contend that it is the most vicious system. That the Brahmins should cultivate knowledge, that the Kshatriya should bear arms, that the Vaishya should trade, and that the Shudra should serve,[100] sounds as though it was a system of division of labour. Whether the theory was intended to state that the Shudra need not, or whether it was intended to lay down that he must not, is an interesting question. The defenders of chaturvarnya give it the first meaning. They say, why need the Shudra trouble to acquire wealth, when the three higher varnas are there to support him? Why need the Shudra bother to take to education, when there is the Brahmin to whom he can go when the occasion for reading or writing arises? Why need the Shudra worry to arm himself, when there is the Kshatriya to protect him? The theory of chaturvarnya, understood in this sense, may be said to look upon the Shudra as the ward and the three higher varnas as his guardians. Thus interpreted, it is a simple, elevating, and alluring theory.

17.2

Assuming this to be the correct view of the underlying conception of chaturvarnya, it seems to me that the system is neither foolproof nor knave-proof. What is to happen if the Brahmins, Vaishyas, and Kshatriyas fail to pursue knowledge, to engage in economic enterprise, and to be efficient soldiers, which are their respective functions? Contrary-wise, suppose that they discharge their functions, but flout their duty to the Shudra or to one another; what is to happen to the Shudra if the three classes refuse to support him on fair terms, or combine to keep him down? Who is to safeguard the interests of the Shudra—or for that matter, those of the Vaishya and Kshatriya— when the person who is trying to take advantage of his ignorance is the Brahmin? Who is to defend the liberty of the Shudra—and for that matter, of the Brahmin and the Vaishya—when the person who is robbing him of it is the Kshatriya?

17.3

Interdependence of one class on another class is inevitable. Even dependence of one class upon another may sometimes become allowable. But why make one person depend upon another in the matter of his vital needs? Education, everyone must have. Means of defence, everyone must have.

These are the paramount requirements of every man for his self-preservation. How can the fact that his neighbour is educated and armed help a man who is uneducated and disarmed? The whole theory is absurd. These are the questions which the defenders of chaturvarnya do not seem to be troubled about. But they are very pertinent questions. Assuming that in their conception of chaturvarnya the relationship between the different classes is that of ward and guardian, and that this is the real conception underlying chaturvarnya, it must be admitted that it makes no provision to safeguard the interests of the ward from the misdeeds of the guardian.

17.4

Whether or not the relationship of guardian and ward was the real underlying conception on which chaturvarnya was based, there is no doubt that in practice the relation was that of master and servants. The three classes, Brahmins, Kshatriyas and Vaishyas, although not very happy in their mutual relationship, managed to work by compromise. The Brahmin flattered the Kshatriya, and both let the Vaishya live in order to be able to live upon him. But the three agreed to beat down the Shudra. He was not allowed to acquire wealth, lest he should be independent of the three varnas. He was prohibited from acquiring knowledge, lest he should keep a steady vigil regarding his interests. He was prohibited from bearing arms, lest he should have the means to rebel against their authority. That this is how the Shudras were treated by the tryavarnikas[101] is evidenced by the laws of Manu. There is no code of laws more infamous regarding social rights than the laws of Manu. Any instance from anywhere of social injustice must pale before it.

17.5

Why have the mass of people tolerated the social evils to which they have been subjected? There have been social revolutions in other countries of the world. Why have there not been social revolutions in India, is a question which has incessantly troubled me. There is only one answer which I can give, and it is that the lower classes of Hindus[102] have been completely disabled for direct action[103] on account of this wretched caste system.[104] They could not bear arms, and without arms they could not rebel. They were all ploughmen— or rather, condemned to be ploughmen— and they never were allowed to convert their ploughshares into swords. They had no bayonets, and therefore everyone who chose, could and did sit upon them. On account of the caste system, they could receive no education. They could not think out or know the way to their salvation. They were condemned to be lowly; and not knowing the way of escape, and not having the means of escape, they became reconciled to eternal servitude,[105] which they accepted as their inescapable fate.

17.6

It is true that even in Europe the strong have not shrunk from the exploitation—nay, the spoliation —of the weak. But in Europe, the strong have never contrived to make the weak helpless against exploitation so shamelessly as was the case in India among the Hindus. Social war has been raging between the strong and the weak far more violently in Europe than it has ever been in India. Yet the weak in Europe has had in his freedom of military service, his physical weapon; in suffering, his political weapon; and in education, his moral weapon. These three weapons for emancipation were never withheld by the strong from the weak in Europe. All these weapons were, however, denied to the masses in India by the caste system.

17.7

There cannot be a more degrading system of social organisation than the caste system. It is the system which deadens, paralyses, and cripples the people, from helpful activity. This is no exaggeration. History bears ample evidence. There is only one period in Indian history which is a period of freedom, greatness and glory. That is the period of the Maurya empire.[107] At all other times the country suffered from defeat and darkness. But the Maurya period was a period when the caste system was completely annihilated—when the Shudras, who constituted the mass of the people, came into their own and became the rulers of the country. The period of defeat and darkness is the period when the caste system flourished, to the damnation of the greater part of the people of the country.

18

18.1

Chaturvarnya is not new. It is as old as the Vedas. That is one of the reasons why we are asked by t he Arya Samajists to consider its claims. Judging from the past, as a system of social organisation it has been tried, and it has failed. How many times have the Brahmins annihilated the seed of the Kshatriyas! How many times have the Kshatriyas annihilated the Brahmins! The Mahabharata and the Puranas are full of incidents of the strife between the Brahmins and the Kshatriyas. They even quarrelled over such petty questions as to who should salute first, as to who should give way first, the Brahmins or the Kshatriyas, when the two met in the street.[108]

18.2

Not only was the Brahmin an eyesore to the Kshatriya and the Kshatriya an eyesore to the Brahmin, it seems that the Kshatriyas had become tyrannical, and the masses, disarmed as they were under the system of chaturvarnya, were praying to almighty god for relief from their tyranny. The Bhagwat[109] tells us very definitely that Krishna had taken avatar for one sacred purpose: and that was, to annihilate the Kshatriyas. With these instances of rivalry and enmity between the different varnas before us, I do not understand how anyone can hold out chaturvarnya as an ideal to be aimed at,[110] or as a pattern on which Hindu society should be remodelled.

19

19.1

I have dealt with those who are without you and whose hostility to your ideal is quite open. There appear to be others who are neither without you nor with you. I was hesitating whether I should deal with their point of view. But on further consideration I have come to the conclusion that I must, and that for two reasons. Firstly, their attitude to the problem of caste is not merely an attitude of neutrality, but is an attitude of armed neutrality.[111] Secondly, they probably represent a considerable body of people. Of these, there is one set which finds nothing peculiar or odious in the caste system of the Hindus. Such Hindus cite the case of Muslims, Sikhs and Christians, and find comfort in the fact that they too have castes amongst them.

19.2

In considering this question, you must at the outset bear in mind that nowhere is human society one single whole.

It is always plural. In the world of action, the individual is one limit and society the other. Between them lie all sorts of associative arrangements of lesser and larger scope—families, friendships, cooperative associations, business combines, political parties, bands of thieves and robbers. These small groups are usually firmly welded together, and are often as exclusive as castes. They have a narrow and intensive code, which is often antisocial. This is true of every society, in Europe as well as in Asia. The question to be asked in determining whether a given society is an ideal society is not whether there are groups in it, because groups exist in all societies.

19.3

The questions to be asked in determining what is an ideal society are: How numerous and varied are the interests which are consciously shared by the groups? How full and free is the interplay with other forms of associations? Are the forces that separate groups and classes more numerous than the forces that unite them? What social significance is attached to this group life? Is its exclusiveness a matter of custom and convenience, or is it a matter of religion? It is in the light of these questions that one must decide whether caste among non-Hindus is the same as caste among Hindus.[112]

19.4

If we apply these considerations to castes among Mahomedans, Sikhs and Christians on the one hand, and to castes among Hindus on the other, you will find that caste among non-Hindus is fundamentally different from caste among Hindus. First, the ties which consciously make the Hindus hold together are non-existent, while among non-Hindus there are many that hold them together. The strength of a society depends upon the presence of points of contact, possibilities of interaction, between different groups which exist in it. These are what Carlyle calls "organic filaments"—i.e., the elastic threads which help to bring the disintegrating elements together and to reunite them.[113] There is no integrating force among the Hindus to counteract the disintegration caused by caste. While among the non-Hindus there are plenty of these "organic filaments" which bind them together.

19.5

Again it must be borne in mind that although there are castes among non-Hindus, as there are among Hindus, caste has not the same social significance for non-Hindus as it has for Hindus. Ask a Mahomedan or a Sikh who he is. He tells you that he is a Mahomedan or a Sikh, as the case may be. He does not tell you his caste although he has one, and you are satisfied with his answer. When he tells you that he is a Muslim, you do not proceed to ask him whether he is a Shia or a Sunni; Sheikh or Saiyad; Khatik or Pinjari.[114] When he tells you he is a Sikh, you do not ask him whether he is Jat or Roda; Mazbi or Ramdasi.[115] But you are not satisfied if a person tells you that he is a Hindu. You feel bound to inquire into his caste. Why? Because so essential is caste in the case of a Hindu that without knowing it you do not feel sure what sort of a being he is.

19.6

That caste has not the same social significance among non-Hindus as it has among Hindus is clear, if you take into consideration the consequences which follow breach of caste. There may be castes among Sikhs and Mahomedans, but the Sikhs and the Mahomedans will not outcast a Sikh or a Mahomedan if he broke his caste. Indeed, the very idea of excommunication is foreign to the Sikhs and the Mahomedans. But with the Hindus the case is entirely different. A Hindu is sure to be outcasted if he broke caste. This shows the difference in the social significance of caste to Hindus and non-Hindus. This is the second point of difference.

19.7

But there is also a third and a more important one. Caste among the non-Hindus has no religious consecration; but among the Hindus most decidedly it has. Among the non-Hindus, caste is only a practice, not a sacred institution. They did not originate it. With them it is only a survival mechanism.[116] They do not regard caste as a religious dogma. Religion compels the Hindus to treat isolation and segregation of castes as a virtue. Religion does not compel the non-Hindus to take the same attitude towards caste. If Hindus wish to break caste, their religion will come in their way. But it will not be so in the case of non-Hindus. It is, therefore, a dangerous delusion to take comfort in the mere existence of caste among non-Hindus, without caring to know what place caste occupies in their life and whether there are other "organic filaments" which subordinate the feeling of caste to the feeling of community. The sooner the Hindus are cured of this delusion, the better.

19.8

The other set denies that caste presents any problem at all for the Hindus to consider. Such Hindus seek comfort in the view that the Hindus have survived, and take this as a proof of their fitness to survive. This point of view is well expressed by Prof S. Radhakrishnan in his Hindu View of Life.[117] Referring to Hinduism, he says:

The civilisation itself has not been a short-lived one. Its historic records date back to over four thousand years and even then it had reached a stage of civilisation which has continued its unbroken, though at times slow and static, course until the present day. It has stood the stress and strain of more than four or five millenniums of spiritual thought and experience. Though peoples of different races and cultures have been pouring into India from the dawn of history, Hinduism has been able to maintain its supremacy and even the proselytising creeds backed by political power have not been able to coerce the large majority of Hindus to their views. The Hindu culture possesses some vitality which seems to be denied to some other more forceful currents. It is no necessary to dissect Hinduism than to open a tree to see whether the sap still runs.

The name of Prof Radhakrishnan is big enough to invest with profundity whatever he says, and impress the minds of his readers.[118] But I must not hesitate to speak out my mind. For I fear that his statement may become the basis of a vicious argument that the fact of survival is proof of fitness to survive.

19.9

It seems to me that the question is not whether a community lives or dies; the question is on what plane does it live. There are different modes of survival. But not all are equally honourable. For an individual as well as for a society, there is a gulf between merely living, and living worthily. To light in a battle and to live in glory is one mode. To beat a retreat, to surrender, and to live the life of a captive is also a mode of survival. It is useless for a Hindu to take comfort in the fact that he and his people have survived. What he must consider is, what is the quality of their survival. If he does that, I am sure he will cease to take pride in the mere fact of survival. A Hindu's life has been a life of continuous defeat, and what appears to him to be life everlasting is not living everlastingly, but is really a life which is perishing everlastingly. It is a mode of survival of which every right-minded Hindu who is not afraid to own up to the truth will feel ashamed.

20

20.1

There is no doubt, in my opinion, that unless you change your social order you can achieve little by way of progress. You cannot mobilise the community either for defence or for offence. You cannot build anything on the foundations of caste. You cannot build up a nation, you cannot build up a morality. Anything that you will build on the foundations of caste will crack, and will never be a whole.

20.2

The only question that remains to be considered is—How to bring about the reform of the Hindu social order? How to abolish caste?[119] This is a question of supreme importance. There is a view that in the reform of caste, the first step to take is to abolish sub-castes. This view is based upon the supposition that there is a greater similarity in manners andstatus between sub-castes than there is between castes. I think this is an erroneous supposition. The Brahmins of northern and central India are socially of lower grade, as compared with the Brahmins of the Deccan and southern India. The former are only cooks and water-carriers, while the latter occupy a high social position. On the other hand, in northern India, the Vaishyas and Kayasthas are intellectually and socially on a par with the Brahmins of the Deccan and southern India.

20.3

Again, in the matter of food there is no similarity between the Brahmins of the Deccan and southern India, who are vegetarians, and the Brahmins of Kashmere and Bengal, who are non- vegetarians. On the other hand, the Brahmins of the Deccan and southern India have more in common so far as food is concerned with such non-Brahmins as the Gujaratis, Marwaris, Banias and Jains.

20.4

There is no doubt that from the standpoint of making the transition[120] from one caste to another easy, the fusion of the Kayasthas of northern India and the other non-Brahmins of southern India with the non-Brahmins of the Deccan and the Dravidian[121] country is more practicable than the fusion of the Brahmins of the south with the Brahmins of the north. But assuming that the fusion of sub-castes is possible, what guarantee is there that the abolition of sub-castes will necessarily lead to the abolition of castes? On the contrary, it may happen that the process may stop with the abolition of sub-castes. In that case, the abolition of sub-castes will only help to strengthen the castes, and make them more powerful and therefore more mischievous. This remedy is therefore neither practicable nor effective, and may easily prove to be a wrong remedy.

20.5

Another plan of action for the abolition of caste is to begin with inter-caste dinners. This also, in my opinion, is an inadequate remedy. There are many castes which allow interdining. But it is a common experience that inter-dining has not succeeded in killing the spirit of caste and the consciousness of caste. I am convinced that the real remedy is intermarriage. Fusion of blood can alone create the feeling of being kith and kin, and unless this feeling of kinship, of being kindred, becomes paramount, the separatist feeling—the feeling of being aliens—created by caste will not vanish. Among the Hindus, intermarriage must necessarily be a factor of greater force in social life than it need be in the life of the non-Hindus. Where society is already well knit by other ties, marriage is an ordinary incident of life. But where society is cut asunder, marriage as a binding force becomes a matter of urgent necessity. The real remedy for breaking caste is intermarriage. Nothing else will serve as the solvent of caste.

20.6

Your Jat-Pat Todak Mandal has adopted this line of attack. It is a direct and frontal attack, and I congratulate you upon a correct diagnosis, and more upon your having shown the courage to tell the Hindus what is really wrong with them. Political tyranny is nothing compared to social tyranny, and a reformer who defies society is a much more courageous man than a politician who defies the government. You are right in holding that caste will cease to be an operative force only when inter-dining and intermarriage have become matters of common course. You have located the source of the disease.

20.7

But is your prescription the right prescription for the disease? Ask yourselves this question: Why is it that a large majority of Hindus do not inter-dine and do not intermarry? Why is it that your cause is not popular?

20.8

There can be only one answer to this question, and it is that inter-dining and intermarriage are repugnant to the beliefs and dogmas which the Hindus regard as sacred. Caste is not a physical object Eke a wall of bricks or a line of barbed wire which prevents the Hindus from commingling and which has, therefore, to be pulled down. Caste is a notion; it is a state of mind. The destruction of caste does not therefore mean the destruction of a physical barrier. It means a notional change.

20.9

Caste may be bad. Caste may lead to conduct so gross as to be called man's inhumanity to man. All the same, it must be recognised that the Hindus observe caste not because they are inhuman or wrong-headed. They observe caste because they are deeply religious. People are not wrong in observing caste. In my view, what is wrong is their religion, which has inculcated this notion of caste. If this is correct, then obviously the enemy you must grapple with is not the people who observe caste, but the shastras which teach them this religion of caste. Criticising and ridiculing people for not inter-dining or intermarrying, or occasionally holding inter-caste dinners and celebrating intercaste marriages, is a futile method of achieving the desired end. The real remedy is to destroy the belief in the sanctity of the shastras.

20.10

How do you expect to succeed if you allow the shastras to continue to mould the beliefs and opinions of the people?

Not to question the authority of the shastras—to permit the people to believe in their sanctity and their sanctions, and then to blame the people and to criticise them for their acts as being irrational and inhuman—is an incongruous way of carrying on social reform. Reformers working for the removal of untouchability, including Mahatma Gandhi, do not seem to realise that the acts of the people are merely the results of their beliefs inculcated in their minds by the shastras, and that people will not change their conduct until they cease to believe in the sanctity of the shastras on which their conduct is founded.

20.11

No wonder that such efforts have not produced any results. You also seem to be erring in the same way as the reformers working in the cause of removing untouchability. To agitate for and to organise inter-caste dinners and inter-caste marriages is like forced feeding brought about by artificial means. Make every man and woman free from the thraldom of the shastras, cleanse their minds of the pernicious notions founded on the shastras, and he or she will inter-dine and intermarry, without your telling him or her to do so.

20.12

It is no use seeking refuge in quibbles. It is no use telling people that the shastras do not say what they are believed to say, if they are grammatically read or logically interpreted. What matters is how the shastras have been understood by the people. You must take the stand that Buddha took. You must take the stand which Guru Nanak took. You must no only discard the shastras, you must deny their authority, as did Buddha and Nanak. You must have courage to tell the

Hindus that what is wrong with them is their religion—the religion which has produced in them this notion of the sacredness of caste. Will you show that courage?

21

21.1

What are your chances of success?[122] Social reforms fall into different species. There is a species of reform which does not relate to the religious notions of a people, but is purely secular in character. There is also a species of reform which relates to the religious notions of a people. Of such a species of reform, there are two varieties. In one, the reform accords with the principles of the religion, and merely invites people who have departed from it, to revert to them and to follow them.

21.2

The second is a reform which not only touches the religious principles but is diametrically opposed to those principles, and invites people to depart from and to discard their authority, and to act contrary to those principles. Caste is the natural outcome of certain religious beliefs which have the sanction of the shastras, which are believed to contain the command of divinely inspired sages who were endowed with a supernatural wisdom and whose commands, therefore, cannot be disobeyed without committing a sin.

21.3

The destruction of caste is a reform which falls under the third category. To ask people to give up caste is to ask them to go contrary to their fundamental religious notions. It is obvious that the first and second species of reform are easy.

But the third is a stupendous task, well-nigh impossible. The Hindus hold to the sacredness of the social order. Caste has a divine basis. You must therefore destroy the sacredness and divinity with which caste has become invested. In the last analysis, this means you must destroy the authority of the shastras and the Vedas.

21.4

I have emphasised this question of the ways and means of destroying caste, because I think that knowing the proper ways and means is more important than knowing the ideal. If you do not know the real ways and means, all your shots are sure to be misfired. If my analysis is correct, then your task is Herculean. You alone can say whether you are capable of achieving it.

21.5

Speaking for myself, I see the task to be well-nigh impossible. Perhaps you would like to know why I think so. Out of the many reasons which have led me to take this view, I will mention some which I regard as most important. One of these reasons is the attitude of hostility which the Brahmins have shown towards this question. The Brahmins form the vanguard of the movement for political reform, and in some cases also of economic reform. But they are not to be found even as camp-followers in the army raised to break down the barricades of caste. Is there any hope of the Brahmins ever taking up a lead in the future in this matter? I say no.

21.6

You may ask why. You may argue that there is no reason why. Brahmins should continue to shun social reform. You may argue that the Brahmins know that the bane of Hindu society is caste, and as an enlightened class they could not be expected to be indifferent to its consequences. You may argue that there are secular Brahmins and priestly Brahmins,[123] and if the latter do not take up the cudgels on behalf of those who want to break caste, the former will.

21.7

All this of course sounds very plausible. But in all this it is forgotten that the break-up of the caste system is bound to adversely affect the Brahmin caste. Having regard to this, is it reasonable to expect that the Brahmins will ever consent to lead a movement, the ultimate result of which is to destroy the power and prestige of the Brahmin caste? Is it reasonable to expect the secular Brahmins to take part in a movement directed against the priestly Brahmins? In my judgement, it is useless to make a distinction between the secular Brahmins and priestly Brahmins. Both are kith and kin. They are two arms of the same body, and one is bound to fight for the existence of the other.

21.8

In this connection, I am reminded of some very pregnant remarks made by Prof Dicey in his English Constitution.[124] Speaking of the actual limitation on the legislative supremacy of parliament, Dicey says: The actual exercise of authority by any sovereign whatever, and notably by Parliament, is bounded or controlled by two limitations. Of these the one is an external, the other is an internal limitation. The external limit to the real power of a sovereign consists in the possibility or certainty that his subjects, or a large number of them, will disobey or resist his laws ...

The internal limit to the exercise of sovereignty arises from the nature of the sovereign power itself. Even a despot exercises his powers in accordance with his character, which is itself moulded by the circumstances under which he lives, including under that head the moral feelings of the time and the society to which he belongs. The Sultan could not, if he would, change the religion of the Mahommedan world, but even if he could do so, it is in the very highest degree improbable that the head of Mahommedanism should wish to overthrow the religion of Mahomet; the internal check on the exercise of the Sultan's power is at least as strong as the external limitation. People sometimes ask the idle question, why the Pope does not introduce this or that reform? The true answer is that a revolutionist is not the kind of man who becomes a Pope, and that the man who becomes a Pope has no wish to be a revolutionist.

21.9

I think these remarks apply equally to the Brahmins of India, and one can say with equal truth that if a man who becomes a Pope has no wish to become a revolutionary, a man who is born a Brahmin has much less desire to become a revolutionary. Indeed, to expect a Brahmin to be a revolutionary in matters of social reform is as idle as to expect the British Parliament, as was said by Leslie Stephen,[125] to pass an Act requiring all blue-eyed babies to be murdered.

21.10

Some of you will say that it is a matter of small concern whether the Brahmins come forward to lead the movement against caste or whether they do not. To take this view is, in my judgement, to ignore the part played by the intellectual class in the community. Whether you accept the theory of the great man as the maker of history[126] or whether you do not, this much you will have to concede: that in every country the intellectual class is the most influential class, if not the governing class. The intellectual class is the class which can foresee, it is the class which can advise and give the lead. In no country does the mass of the people live the life of intelligent thought and action. It is largely imitative, and follows the intellectual class.

21.11

There is no exaggeration in saying that the entire destiny of a country depends upon its intellectual class. If the intellectual class is honest, independent and disinterested, it can be trusted to take the initiative and give a proper lead when a crisis arises. It is true that intellect by itself is no virtue. It is only a means, and the use of means depends upon the ends which an intellectual person pursues. An intellectual man can be a good man, but he can easily be a rogue. Similarly an intellectual class may be a band of high-souled persons, ready to help, ready to emancipate erring humanity—or it may easily be a gang of crooks, or a body of advocates for a narrow clique from which it draws its support.

21.12

You may think it a pity that the intellectual class in India is simply another name for the Brahmin caste. You may regret that the two are one; that the existence of the intellectual class should be bound up with one single caste; that this intellectual class should share the interest and the aspirations of that Brahmin caste, which has regarded itself as the custodian of the interest of that caste rather than of the interests of the country. All this may be very regrettable. But the fact remains that the Brahmins form the intellectual class of the Hindus. It is not only an intellectual class, but it is a class which is held in great reverence by the rest of the Hindus.

21.13

The Hindus are taught that the Brahmins are Bhu-devas (gods on earth).[127] The Hindus are taught that Brahmins alone can be their teachers. Manu says: If it be asked how it should be with respect to points of the Dharma which have not been specially mentioned, the answer is, that which Brahmins who are shishthas propound shall doubtless have legal forced.[1]

21.14

When such an intellectual class, which holds the rest of the community in its grip, is opposed to the reform of caste, the chances of success in a movement for the break-up of the caste system appear to me very, very remote.

21.15

The second reason why I say the task is impossible will be clear, if you will bear in mind that the caste system has two aspects. In one of its aspects, it divides men into separate communities. In its second aspect, it places these communities in a graded order one above the other in social status. Each caste takes its pride and its consolation in the fact that in the scale of castes it is above some other caste. As an outward mark of this gradation, there is also a gradation of social and religious rights, technically spoken of as ashtadhikaras[130] and sanskaras.[131] The higher the grade of a caste, the greater the number of these rights; and the lower the grade, the lesser their number.

21.16

Now this gradation, this scaling of castes, makes it impossible to organise a common front against the caste system. If a caste claims the right to inter-dine and intermarry with another caste placed above it, it is frozen the instant it is told[132] by mischief-mongers—and there are many Brahmins amongst such mischief-mongers—that it will have to concede inter-dining and intermarriage with castes below it! All are slaves of the caste system. But all the slaves are not equal in status.[133]

21.17

To excite the proletariat to bring about an economic revolution, Karl Marx told them: "You have nothing to lose except your chains."[134] But the artful way in which the social and religious rights are distributed among the different castes, whereby some have more and some have less, makes the slogan of Karl Marx quite useless[135] to excite the Hindus against the caste system. Castes form a graded system of sovereignties, high and low, which are jealous of their status and which know that if a general dissolution came, some of them stand to lose more of their prestige and power than others do.[136] You cannot, therefore, have a general mobilisation of the Hindus (to use a military expression) for an attack on the caste system.

22

22.1

Can you appeal to reason, and ask the Hindus to discard caste as being contrary to reason? That raises the question:

Is a Hindu free to follow his reason? Manu has laid down three sanctions to which every Hindu must conform in the matter of his behaviour:

22.2

Here there is no place for reason to play its part. A Hindu must follow either Veda, smriti or sadachar.[138] He cannot follow anything else.

22.3

In the first place, how are the texts of the Vedas and smritis to be interpreted whenever any doubt arises regarding their meaning? On this important question the view of Manu is quite definite. He says:

22.4

According to this rule, rationalism as a canon of interpreting the Vedas and smritis is absolutely condemned. It is regarded to be as wicked as atheism, and the punishment provided for it is excommunication. Thus, where a matter is covered by the Veda or the smriti, a Hindu cannot resort to rational thinking.

22.5

Even when there is a conflict between Vedas and smritis on matters on which they have given a positive injunction, the solution is not left to reason. When there is a conflict between two shrutis, both are to be regarded as of equal authority. Either of them may be followed. No attempt[141] is to be made to find out which of the two accords with reason. This is made clear by Manu: When there is a conflict between shruti and smriti, the shruti must prevail. But here too no attempt must be made to find out which of the two accords with reason. This is laid down by Manu in the following shloka:

22.6

Again, when there is a conflict between two smritis, the Manusmriti must prevail, but no attempt is to be made to find out which of the two accords with reason. This is the ruling given by Brihaspati:[144]

22.7

It is therefore clear that in any matter on which the shrutis and smritis have given a positive direction, a Hindu is not free to use his reasoning faculty. The same rule is laid down in the Mahabharata:

22.8

He must abide by their directions. Caste and varna are matters which are dealt with by the Vedas and the smritis, and consequently, appeal to reason can have no effect on a Hindu.

22.9

So far as caste and varna are concerned, not only the shastras do not permit the Hindu to use his reason in the decision of the question, but they have taken care to see that no occasion is left to examine in a rational way the foundations of his belief in caste and varna. It must be a source of silent amusement to many a non-Hindu to find hundreds and thousands of Hindus breaking caste on certain occasions, such as railway journeys and foreign travel, and yet endeavouring to maintain caste for the rest of their lives!

22.10

The explanation of this phenomenon discloses another fetter on the reasoning faculties of the Hindus. Man's life is generally habitual and unreflective. Reflective thought—in the sense of active, persistent, and careful consideration of any belief or supposed form of knowledge, in the light of the grounds that support it and the further conclusions to which it tends—is quite rare, and arises only in a situation which presents a dilemma or a crisis. Railway journeys and foreign travels are really occasions of crisis in the life of a Hindu, and it is natural to expect a Hindu to ask himself why he should maintain caste at all, if he cannot maintain it at all times. But he does not. He breaks caste at one step, and proceeds to observe it at the next, without raising any question.[147]

22.11

The reason for this astonishing conduct is to be found in the rule of the shastras, which directs him to maintain caste as far as possible and to undergo prayaschitta[148] when he cannot. By this theory of prayaschitta, the shastras, by following a spirit of compromise, have given caste a perpetual lease on life, and have smothered the reflective thought which would have otherwise led to the destruction of the notion of caste.[149]

22.12

There have been many who have worked in the cause of the abolition of caste and untouchability. Of those who can be mentioned, Ramanuja,[150] Kabir,[151] and others stand out prominently. Can you appeal to the acts of these reformers and exhort the Hindus to follow them?

22.13

It is true that Manu has included (sadachar) as one of the sanctions along with shruti and smriti. Indeed, sadachar has been given a higher place than shastras:

22.14

According to this, sadachar, whether it is or[153] in accordance with shastras or contrary to shastras, must be followed. But what is the meaning of sadachar? If anyone were to suppose that sadachar means right or good acts—i.e., acts of good and righteous men—he would find himself greatly mistaken. Sadachar does not mean good acts or acts of good men. It means ancient custom, good or bad. The following verse makes this clear:

22.15

As though to warn people against the view that sadachar means good acts or acts of good men, and fearing that people might understand it that way and follow the acts of good men, the smritis have commanded the Hindus in unmistakable terms not to follow even gods in their good deeds, if they are contrary to shruti, smriti and sadachar. This may sound to be most extraordinary, most perverse, but the fact remains that[155] is an injunction issued to the Hindus by their shastras.

22.16

Reason and morality are the two most powerful weapons in the armoury of a reformer. To deprive him of the use of these weapons is to disable him for action. How are you going to break up caste, if people are not free to consider whether it accords with reason? How are you going to break up caste, if people are not free to consider whether it accords with morality? The wall built around caste is impregnable, and the material of which it is built contains none of the combustible stuff of reason and morality. Add to this the fact that inside this wall stands the army of Brahmins who form the intellectual class, Brahmins who are the natural leaders of the Hindus, Brahmins who are there not as mere mercenary soldiers but as an army fighting for its homeland, and you will get an idea why I think that the breaking up of caste among the Hindus is well-nigh impossible. At any rate, it would take ages before a breach is made.

22.17

But whether the doing of the deed takes time or whether it can be done quickly, you must not forget that if you wish to bring about a breach in the system, then you have got to apply the dynamite to the Vedas and the shastras, which deny any part to reason; to the Vedas and shastras, which deny any part to morality. You must destroy the religion of the shrutis and the smritis. Nothing else will avail. This is my considered view of the matter.

23

23.1

Some may not understand what I mean by destruction of religion, some may find the idea revolting to them, and some may find it revolutionary. Let me therefore explain my position. I do not know whether you draw a distinction between principles and rules. But I do. Not only do I make a distinction, but I say that this distinction is real and important. Rules are practical; they are habitual ways of doing things according to prescription. But principles are intellectual; they are useful methods of judging things. Rules seek to tell an agent just what course of action to pursue. Principles do not prescribe a specific course of action. Rules, like cooking recipes, do tell just what to do and how to do it. A principle, such as that of justice, supplies a main heading by reference to which he is to consider the bearings of his desires and purposes; it guides him in his thinking by suggesting to him the important consideration which he should bear in mind.

23.2

This difference between rules and principles makes the acts done in pursuit of them different in quality and in content.[156] Doing what is said to be good by virtue of a rule and doing good in the light of a principle are two different things. The principle may be wrong, but the act is conscious and responsible. The rule may be right, but the act is mechanical. A religious act may not be a correct act, but must at least be a responsible act. To permit of this responsibility, religion must mainly be a matter of principles only. It cannot be a matter of rules. The moment it degenerates into rules it ceases to be religion, as it kills the responsibility which is the essence of a truly religious act.

23.3

What is this Hindu religion? Is it a set of principles, or is it a code of rules? Now the Hindu religion, as contained in the Vedas and the smritis, is nothing but a mass of sacrificial, social, political, and sanitary rules and regulations, all mixed up. What is called religion by the Hindus is nothing but a multitude of commands and prohibitions. Religion, in the sense of spiritual principles, truly universal, applicable to all races, to all countries, to all times, is not to be found in them; and if it is, it does not form the governing part of a Hindu's life. That for a Hindu dharma means commands and prohibitions is clear from the way the word dharma is used in the Vedas and the smritis and understood by the commentators. The word dharma as used in the Vedas in most cases means religious ordinances or rites. Even Jaimini in his Purva Mimamsa[157] defines dharma as "a desirable goal or result that is indicated by injunctive (Vedic) passages".

23.4

To put it in plain language, what the Hindus call religion is really law, or at best legalised class-ethics. Frankly, I refuse to call this code of ordinances as religion. The first evil of such a code of ordinances, misrepresented to the people as religion, is that it tends to deprive moral life of freedom and spontaneity, and to reduce it (for the conscientious, at any rate) to a more or less anxious and servile conformity to externally imposed rules. Under it, there is no loyalty to ideals; there is only conformity to commands.

23.5

But the worst evil of this code of ordinances is that the laws it contains must be the same yesterday, today and forever. They are iniquitous in that they are not the same for one class as for another. But this iniquity is made perpetual in that they are prescribed to be the same for all generations. The objectionable part of such a scheme is not that they are made by certain persons called prophets or law-givers. The objectionable part is that this code has been invested with the character of finality and fixity. Happiness notoriously varies with the conditions and circumstances of a person, as well as with the conditions of different people and epochs. That being the case, how can humanity endure this code of eternal laws, without being cramped and without being crippled?

23.6

I have, therefore, no hesitation in saying that such a religion must be destroyed, and I say there is nothing irreligious in working for the destruction of such a religion. Indeed I hold that it is your bounden duty to tear off the mask, to remove the misrepresentation that is caused by misnaming this law as religion. This is an essential step for you. Once you clear the minds of the people of this misconception and enable them to realise that what they are told is religion is not religion, but that it is really law, you will be in a position to urge its amendment or abolition.

23.7

So long as people look upon it as religion they will not be ready for a change, because the idea of religion is generally speaking not associated with the idea of change. But the idea of law is associated with the idea of change, and when people come to know that what is called religion is really law, old and archaic, they will be ready for a change, for people know and accept that law can be changed.

24

24.1

While I condemn a religion of rules, I must not be understood to hold the opinion that there is no necessity for a religion. On the contrary, I agree with Burke when he says that "True religion is the foundation of society, the basis on which all true Civil Government rests, and both their sanction."[158] Consequently, when I urge that these ancient rules of life be annulled, I am anxious that their place shall be taken by a religion of principles, which alone can lay claim to being a true religion. Indeed, I am so convinced of the necessity of religion that I feel I ought to tell you in outline what I regard as necessary items in this religious reform. The following, in my opinion, should be the cardinal items in this reform:

1. There should be one and only one standard book of Hindu religion, acceptable to all Hindus and recognised by all Hindus. This of course means that all other books of Hindu religion such as Vedas, shastras, and puranas, which are treated as sacred and authoritative, must by law cease to be so, and the preaching of any doctrine, religious or social, contained in these books should be penalized.
2. It would be better if priesthood among Hindus were abolished. But as this seems to be impossible, the priesthood must at least cease to be hereditary. Every person who professes to be a Hindu must be eligible for being a priest. It should be provided by law that no Hindu shall be entitled to be a priest unless he has passed an examination prescribed by the state, and holds a sanad[159] from the state him to practise.
3. No ceremony performed by a priest who does not hold a sanad shall be deemed to be valid in law, and it should be made penal for a person who has no sanad to officiate as a priest.
4. A priest should be the servant of the state,[160] and should be subject to the disciplinary action of the state in the matter of his morals, beliefs, and worship, in addition to his being subject along with other citizens to the ordinary law of the land.
5. The number of priests should be limited by law according to the requirements of the state, as is done in the case of the ICS [Indian Civil Service].

24.2

To some, this may sound radical. But to my mind there is nothing revolutionary in this. Every profession in India is regulated. Engineers must show proficiency, doctors must show proficiency, lawyers must show proficiency, before they are allowed to practise their professions. During the whole of their career, they must not only obey the law of the land, civil as well as criminal, but they must also obey the special code of morals prescribed by their respective professions. The priest's is the only profession where proficiency is not required. The profession of a Hindu priest is the only profession which is not subject to any code.

24.3

Mentally a priest may be an idiot, physically a priest may be suffering from a foul disease such as syphilis or gonorrhoea, morally he may be a wreck. But he is fit to officiate at solemn ceremonies, to enter the sanctum sanctorum of a Hindu temple, and to worship the Hindu god. All this becomes possible among the Hindus because for a priest it is enough to be born in a priestly caste. The whole thing is abominable, and is due to the fact that the priestly class among Hindus is subject neither to law nor to morality. It recognises no duties. It knows only of rights and privileges. It is a pest which divinity seems to have let loose on the masses for their mental and moral degradation.

24.4

The priestly class must be brought under control by some such legislation as I have outlined above. This will prevent it from doing mischief and from misguiding people. It will democratise it by throwing it open to everyone. It will certainly help to kill Brahminism and will also help to kill caste, which is nothing but Brahminism incarnate. Brahminism is the poison which has spoiled Hinduism. You will succeed in saving Hinduism if you will kill Brahminism. There should be no opposition to this reform from any quarter. It should be welcomed even by the Arya Samajists, because this is merely an application of their own doctrine of guna—karma.[161]

24.5

Whether you do that or you do not, you must give a new doctrinal basis to your religion—a basis that will be in consonance with liberty, equality and fraternity; in short, with democracy. I am no authority on the subject. But I am told that for such religious principles as will be in consonance with liberty, equality and fraternity, it may not be necessary for you to borrow from foreign sources, and that you could draw for such principles on the Upanishads. Whether you could do so without a complete remoulding, a considerable scraping and chipping off from the ore they contain, is more than I can say. This means a complete change in the fundamental notions of life. It means a complete change in the values of life. It means a complete change in outlook and in attitude towards men and things.

24.6

It means conversion; but if you do not like the word, I will say it means new life. But a new life cannot enter a body that is dead. New life can enter only into a new body. The old body must die before a new body can come into existence and a new life can enter into it. To put it simply: the old must cease to be operative before the new can begin to enliven and to pulsate. This is what I meant when I said you must discard the authority of the shastras, and destroy the religion of the shastras.

25

25.1

I have kept you too long. It is time I brought this address to a close. This would have been a convenient point for me to have stopped. But this would probably be my last address to a Hindu audience, on a subject vitally concerning the Hindus. I would therefore like, before I close, to place before the Hindus, if they will allow me, some questions which I regard as vital, and invite them seriously to consider the same.

25.2

In the first place, the Hindus must consider whether it is sufficient to take the placid view of the anthropologist that there is nothing to be said about the beliefs, habits, morals and outlooks on life which obtain among the different peoples of the world, except that they often differ; or whether it is not necessary to make an attempt to find out what kind of morality, beliefs, habits, and outlook have worked best and have enabled those who possessed them to flourish, to grow strong, to people the earth and to have dominion over it. As is observed by Professor Carver:

Morality and religion, as the organised expression of moral approval and disapproval, must be regarded as factors in the struggle for existence as truly as are weapons for offence and defence, teeth and claws, horns and hoofs, fur and feathers, plumage, beards, and antlers. The social group, community, tribe or nation which develops an unworkable scheme of morality, or within which those social acts which weaken it and unfit it for survival habitually create the sentiment of approval, while those which would strengthen it and enable it to expand habitually create the sentiment of disapproval, will eventually be eliminated. Its habits of approval and disapproval handicap it as really as the possession of two wings on one side with none on the other would handicap a colony of flies. It would be as futile in one case as in the other to argue that one system was just as good as another.[162]

25.3

Morality and religion, therefore, are not mere matters of likes and dislikes. You may dislike exceedingly a scheme of morality which, if universally practised within a nation, would make that nation the strongest nation on the face of the earth. Yet in spite of your dislike, such a nation will become strong. You may like exceedingly a scheme of morality and an ideal of justice which, if universally practised within a nation, would make it unable to hold its own in the struggle with other nations. Yet in spite of your admiration, this nation will eventually disappear. The Hindus must, therefore, examine their religion and their morality in terms of their survival value.

25.4

Secondly, the Hindus must consider whether they should conserve the whole of their social heritage, or select what is helpful and transmit to future generations only that much and no more. Prof John Dewey, who was my teacher and to whom I owe so much, has said:

> Every society gets encumbered with what is trivial, with dead wood from the past, and with what is positively perverse ... As a society becomes more enlightened, it realises that it

is responsible not to conserve and transmit the whole of its existing achievements, but only such as make for a better future society.

Even Burke, in spite of the vehemence with which he opposed the principle of change embodied in the French Revolution, was compelled to admit that a State without the means of some change is without the means of its conservation. Without such means it might even risk the loss of that part of the constitution which it wished the most religiously to preserve.

What Burke said of a state applies equally to society.

25.5

Thirdly, the Hindus must consider whether they must not cease to worship the past as supplying their ideals. The baneful effects of this worship of the past are best summed up by Prof Dewey when he says:

An individual can live only in the present. The present is not just something which comes after the past; much less something produced by it. It is what life is in leaving the[107] past behind it. The study of past products will not help us to understand the present. A knowledge of the past and its heritage is of great significance when it enters into the present, but not otherwise. And the mistake of making the records and remains of the past the main material of education is that it tends to make the past a rival of the present and the present a more or less futile imitation of the past.

The principle, which makes little of the present act of living and growing, naturally looks upon the present as empty and upon the future as remote. Such a principle is inimical to progress and is a hindrance to a strong and a steady current of life.

25.6

Fourthly, the Hindus must consider whether the time has not come for them to recognise that there is nothing fixed, nothing eternal, nothing sanatan;[166] that everything is changing, that change is the law of life for individuals as well as for society. In a changing society, there must be a constant revolution of old values; and the Hindus must realise that if there must be standards to measure the acts of men, there must also be a readiness to revise those standards.

26

26.1

I have to confess that this address has become too lengthy. Whether this fault is compensated to any extent by breadth or depth is a matter for you to judge. All I claim is to have told you candidly my views. I have little to recommend them but some study and a deep concern in your destiny. If you will allow me to say it, these views are the views of a man who has been no tool of power, no flatterer of greatness. They come from one, almost the whole of whose public exertion has been one continuous struggle for liberty for the poor and for the oppressed, and whose only reward has been a continuous shower of calumny and abuse from national journals and national leaders,[167] for no other reason except that I refuse to join with them in performing the miracle—I will not say trick—of liberating the oppressed with the gold of the tyrant, and raising the poor with the cash of the rich.

26.2

All this may not be enough to commend my views. I think they are not likely to alter yours. But whether they do or do not, the responsibility is entirely yours. You must make your efforts to uproot caste, if not in my way, then in your way.

26.3

I am sorry, I will not be with you. I have decided to change. This is not the place for giving reasons. But even when I am gone out of your fold, I will watch your movement with active sympathy, and you will have my assistance for what it may be worth. Yours is a national cause. Caste is no doubt primarily the breath of the Hindus. But the Hindus have fouled the air all over, and everybody is infected—Sikh, Muslim and Christian.[168] You, therefore, deserve the support of all those who are suffering from this infection—Sikh, Muslim and Christian.

26.4

Yours is more difficult than the other national cause, namely, swaraj.[169] In the fight for swaraj you fight with the whole nation on your side. In this, you have to fight against the whole nation—and that too, your own.[170] But it is more important than swaraj. There is no use having swaraj, if you cannot defend it. More important than the question of defending swaraj is the question of defending the Hindus under the swaraj. In my opinion, it is only when Hindu society becomes a casteless society that it can hope to have strength enough to defend itself. Without such internal strength, swaraj for Hindus may turn out to be only a step towards slavery. Goodbye, and good wishes for your success.

Notes

1. "Varnanam Brahmano Guru." This is Manusmriti 10.3. Bibek Debroy's translation: "Among varnas, the Brahman is the teacher/preceptor." There is no standardised text of the Manusmriti;

in some versions, the text mentions prabhu (lord) instead of guru (teacher). George B□hler renders the entire couplet at 10.3 as follows: "On account of his pre-eminence, on account of the superiority of his origin, on account of his observance of (particular) restrictive rules, and on account of his particular sanctification the Brahmana is the lord of (all) castes (varna)" (1886/2004, 276). Chapter 10 of the Manusmriti discusses varnas and their duties at length and lists out dos and don'ts.

2. Ramdas (1608—81) was a seventeenth-century coeval of the Maratha king Shivaji (1627/30-80) is said to have been his Brahmin guru. Bhakti poet Tukaram, Shudra by birth and trader by profession, was also his contemporary. Bhakti is devotional love for a personal god experienced without the mediation of the priest or ritual. The progenitors of the Bhakti movement, the Alvars (sixth to ninth centuries) and Nayanmars (twelfth century) of the Tamil country, were fiercely monotheistic in their expression of love for Vishnu and Siva or their forms, and this happened at the expense and persecution of Jains and Buddhists (see Monius 2011). What was crucial, however, was that anyone from any strata of society—men and women—could aspire to reach god. The twelfth-century Basava-led Veerashaiva movement in the Kannada-speaking South, that launched the literary vachana tradition, repudiated the caste system and the primacy of the Brahmin. Between the fourteenth and eighteenth centuries, sometimes fusing with elements of Islam and Sufism, the Bhakti movement manifested itself variously in the western, northern and eastern parts of the subcontinent through the work of sants, or teachers, who were largely from working-caste backgrounds but also included Brahmins (like Dnyaneshwar in western India or Chaitanya in Bengal) who embraced Bhakti's egalitarian credo. According to the scholar Veena Naregal (2001, 12), Ramdas's "religious and political pragmatism were quite at variance with the inspiration of the Bhakti poets". Dasbodh, composed of 70,000 ovis over twenty sections, offers an interpretation of vedantic philosophy. Ramdas talked of the need for the return of Brahmin supremacy and viewed the crisis in Maratha society as a breakdown in the social order due to 'Muslim oppression', Hindu conversions to Islam, and the usurpation of Brahmin spiritual leadership by the non-

Brahmin Varkari saints and gurus (Ranade 1983). Ramdas today is a hero for Hindu nationalists, especially the Chitpavan Brahmins of Maharashtra. See also Note 32 on the Varkari tradition. Also see Gail Omvedt's account (1976) of the differences between Mahanubhav Bhakti and Ramdas's version of it, which she argues blunted the radical potential of Mahanubhav.

3. Antyaja: last-born; a term used for those outside the pale of the fourfold varna system which comprises Brahmin (priests), Kshatriya (warriors), Vaishya (merchants and farmers) and Shudra (menials). Of these, the first three groups are considered dwija, twice-born. The Shudra are the servile class meant to serve the top three varnas. The antyaja are outside the pale— Untouchables meant to live outside the village.
4. Savarna: those with varna, a caste Hindu; a term used for those within the fourfold varna system Shudra is also a savarna; the opposite of savarna is avarna, the Untouchable.
5. "Heart-burning" in AoC 1936 and subsequent editions.
6. Ambedkar is borrowing this term from John Dewey (1859—1952), the prominent American pragmatist philosopher, radical democrat and educational theorist who taught Ambedkar at Columbia University and influenced him deeply. Dewey, author of about forty books, helped create some of the most prominent political and educational organisations of his time: the American Civil Liberties Union, the National Association for the Advancement of Colored People (NAACP), the League for Industrial Democracy, the New York Teachers Union, the American Association of University Professors, and the New School for Social Research. "Social efficiency" was a term that began its career in 1884 when it was introduced by British sociologist Benjamin Kidd (known for his work Social Evolution, 1884) who used it in a social Darwinist sense, but Dewey and others sought to rescue the term from a narrow, utilitarian approach and imbue it with humanitarian value. In the field of education, the term acquired currency in the 1920s. Arun P. Mukherjee (2009), who offers a fine analysis of Ambedkar's refashioning of Deweyan thought into a tool for his own investigations of Indian society, argues that for Dewey and Ambedkar social efficiency lies in the individual being able to choose and develop his/her competencies

to the fullest and thus mindfully contribute to the functioning of society. For a system that predetermines a person's occupation on the basis of caste or class affiliations cannot but result in inefficiency. The term has its origins in early- twentieth-century attempts at reorganising society, politics and the economy for 'efficiency' based on 'scientific principles'. For more on this, see Knoll (2009) and Holt (1994).

7. The (Indian National) Social Conference was founded by Mahadev Govind Ranade (1842—190 1887, two years after the founding of the Indian National Congress. It was meant to serve as the social arm of the Congress, and it focused mainly on women's uplift. Conservative leaders like B.G. Tilak were staunchly opposed to even the mild reforms suggested by votaries of the Social Conference.
8. Bal Gangadhar 'Lokmanya' Tilak (1865-1920) was a Chitpavan Brahmin and a social conserva who sought to imbue Congress nationalism with a distinct right-wing hue. He published two newspapers, the Marathi-language Kesari and Mahratta in English. Jaffrelot (2005, 44) calls him "the Congress leader from Poona who tended not to put in practice the social reforms he articulated" (emphasis added). Tilak saw even the education of women and non-Brahmins as "a loss of nationality" and consistently opposed the establishment of girls' schools at a time when his coeval Jotiba Phule launched a full-scale attack on Brahminism, educated his wife Savitri, and established a school for girls which also admitted Untouchable children. See Rao (n.d.). For an account of the Phule-led non-Brahmin movement, see O'Hanlon (2002).
9. For a chronicle of the tussles between the Social Conference and conservative forces within the Congress, see John R. McLane (1988, 47—61). McLane writes: "In Maharashtra, Tilak demonstrated the potent political appeal of Hindu symbolism with the Ganapati and Shivaji festivals. In 1895, when the Congress met in Poona, the rowdyism of Tilak's anti-reformer allies forced the Social Conference to abandon the use of the Congress enclosure for its meeting" (55).
10. Womesh Chunder Bonnerjee was amongst the founders of the Indian National Congress and became its first president. As a lawyer, he divided his life between England and Calcutta, and

on retirement settled in Croydon, England. See the account of his daughter Janaki Agnes Penelope Majumdar (2003). While studying in England, in 1865, Bonnerjee wrote in a letter to his uncle: "I have discarded all ideas of caste, I have come to hate all the demoralising practices of our countrymen and I write this letter an entirely altered man" (Kumar 1989, 48). Since he had 'lost caste' by crossing the seas, Bonnerjee was regarded an outcaste by his family. He set up a separate household refusing to undergo penance, and renounced Hindu customs. He brought his wife out of purdah, made her eat beef and wear English clothes, and sent his children to England for education (Majumdar 2003).

11. The Peshwas were initially ministers under Shivaji who founded the Maratha empire in seventeenth-century western India. After the death of Shivaji in 1680, the Peshwas, who were Chitpavan Brahmins, turned into a military-bureaucratic elite, and, in one of those rare instances, both ritual and secular power were vested with Brahmins. The reign of the Peshwas witnessed what feminist scholar Uma Chakravarti (1995, 3—21) terms "the consolidation of Brahmanya-raj". In 1818, the 30,000-strong army of the last Peshwa, Bajirao II (1795-1818), was defeated by the 500-member regiment of 'Untouchable' Mahar soldiers led by Capt F.F. Staunton. This is known as the Battle of Koregaon, along the river Bhima, northwest of Poona. For an account of the rise of the Brahmins in western India, see Eaton (2005).
12. In large parts of India, Dalit women act as dais (midwives) and are expected to help with childbirth in privileged-caste households.
13. Ambedkar is referring here to the court of Indore. This can be inferred from a citation of the sam Times of India article in the posthumously published Untouchables or the Children of India's Ghetto (BAWS 5, 48—9).
14. Following a Bombay government ruling, in August 1935, that Untouchable students should be admitted to schools, the Untouchables of Kavitha village enrolled four children in the local school. This invoked both physical assaults and social boycott, and the Untouchables turned to the Harijan Sevak Sangh, an organisation founded by M.K. Gandhi, for help. Gandhi and 'Sardar' Vallabhbhai Patel opposed the Untouchables' efforts at taking recourse to law, and forced them to withdraw their

complaint. Ambedkar, while recounting this incident, does not mince words (BAWS 5, 43): "With all the knowledge of tyranny and oppression practised by the caste Hindus of Kavitha against the Untouchables all that Mr Gandhi felt like doing was to advise the Untouchables to leave the village. He did not even suggest that the miscreants should be hauled up before a court of law. His henchman, Mr Vallabhbhai Patel, played a part which was still more strange. He had gone to Kavitha to persuade the caste Hindus not to molest the Untouchables. But they did not even give him a hearing. Yet this very man was opposed to the Untouchables hauling them up in a court of law and getting them punished. The Untouchables filed the complaint notwithstanding his opposition. But he ultimately forced them to withdraw the complaint on the caste Hindus making some kind of a show of an understanding not to molest, an undertaking, which the Untouchables can never enforce. The result was that the Untouchables suffered and their tyrants escaped with the aid of Mr Gandhi's friend, Mr Vallabhbhai Patel."

15. "Ran away" in AoC 1936 and subsequent editions.
16. The state of affairs in Chakwara has far from improved. Dalits in this village, denied access to t local pond, have been waging a struggle since 1980. In 2001, two Dalits were fined Rs 50,000 by the Jat- and Brahmin-dominated village panchayat for using water from the Chakwara pond (Usmani, 2008).
17. John Stuart Mill (1806—73) in the last chapter of Considerations on Representative Governme (1861/2004) poses a critique of the colonial administration of the British empire. However, Mill's criticism has to be seen in the context of his advocating "representative government" for the Americas and Australia for they are "composed of people of similar civilisation to the ruling country", and "whose population", he says, "is in a sufficiently advanced state", compared to which "others, like India, are still at a great distance from that state". Here, Mill argues, the coloniser must rule to introduce a higher form of civilisation. Ambedkar is alluding here to his contemporaries' reverence for a complex figure who on the one hand championed the cause of individual freedom and liberty, and on the other, defended British imperialism by justifying the right of 'civilised' nations to rule over 'barbarians'.

In his essay "A Few Words on Non-Intervention" (1859/1984), Mill outlines the circumstances under which states should be allowed to intervene in the sovereign affairs of another country.

18. Term added in 1937.
19. Ferdinand Lassalle (1825—64) was a philologist, legal expert and social agitator, the first to organise a socialist party in Germany and rally the workers to assert their rights. He came to prominence as an interpreter of Marxism for the workers. However, from a letter written by Marx to Ludwig Kugelmann on 23 February 1865 it is clear that Marx considered Lassalle's interpretation plagiarism. In the same letter he also expresses his condemnation of Lassalle's attempt at striking a deal with Bismarck urging him to introduce universal adult suffrage in exchange of working-class support for the government.
20. Ambedkar is quoting from "On the Essence of Constitutions", the famous speech Lassalle delive on 16 April 1862 in Berlin.
21. Rendered as "Lasalle" in AoC 1936.
22. The Communal Award, also known as the Ramsay Macdonald Award after the British Prime Minister, issued on 16 August 1932, was the result of the Second Round Table Conference (September—December 1931) that granted separate electorates to minorities in the dominion of India. Besides Muslims and Sikhs, the Depressed Classes were also granted a separate electorate for twenty years. The award granted a double vote to Untouchables that allowed them to choose their own representatives from special constituencies, as well as to cast their vote in general constituencies. The Congress and Gandhi opposed this, and Gandhi went on indefinite hunger strike in Poona jail. A compromise was reached with the signing of the Poona Pact on 24 September 1932, under which the Untouchables were allotted reserved constituencies but not separate electorates. See the text of the Communal Award in B.R. Ambedkar (BAWS 9, 81). For a further delineation of the Communal Award and the Poona Pact and their implications, see "A Note on the Poona Pact" in this book (357—76).
23. For an analysis and discussion of the Communal Award and the Poona Pact, see Zelliot (2013, 128—42); Jaffrelot (2005, 52-73); Kumar (1985).

24. The Irish Home Rule movement was launched in the second half of the nineteenth century to recover legislative independence from the British after Ireland had become part of the Union. See more in Alan O'Day (1998) and AlvinJackson (2003). Howard Brasted (1980) argues that the precedent of the Irish Home Rule movement awoke the nationalist spirit amongst the educated Indian elite and provided a model for the Congress. Home Rule could never be implemented in Ireland due to the strong oppostion by the Protestant Unionists of Northern Ireland (Ulstermen). Here, it is not clear if Ambedkar is referring to John Edward Redmond (1856-1918), Member of Parliament and leader of the Irish Parliamentary Party and the National League, or his brother, William (Willie) Redmond (1861-1917), also an MP and nationalist politician.
25. Pontifex Maximus was the highest priest of the college of pontiffs in ancient Rome.
26. Patricians (derived from the root patre, meaning 'father') were the upper class in ancient Rome Their ancestry was traced back by Roman historians such as Livy to the legend of Romulus, the mythical founder of Rome, who is said to have appointed one hundred men as senators. Patricians claimed to be descendants of these first senators and the Sabine women kidnapped and raped for procreation. Plebeians were the general body of lower-class, free citizens. There were other lower classes like the peregrini and slaves. Most historians agree that the distinction between patricians, plebeians and other classes was based purely on birth. The most readily available tool to distinguish between the classes was gentes, family names. See Livy (2006).
27. In his speech during the second leg of the Mahad Satyagraha on 25 December 1927, Ambedkar refers to the patrician-plebeian struggle, or 'the Conflict of the Orders' as it is more commonly known, in greater detail. The Conflict of the Orders, in which the plebeians sought political equality with the patricians, lasted between 494 and 287 BCE. In this protracted conflict, the patricians were occasionally forced to give some concession to the plebeians, but always sought to retain the final authority. Thus the provisions for economic reform in laws like Lex Licinia Sextia (367

BCE) and Leges Genuciae (342 BCE)—ceiling on the ownership of land by a single person, ban on lending that carried interest, etc.—were largely ignored by the patricians. In his Mahad speech, Ambedkar gives a very interesting account of how the positions of 'tribunes', constituted to protect the rights of the plebeians, were held exclusively by patricians in the beginning. Even when later laws stipulated that one of the two tribunes must be a plebeian, the patricians retained the power to reject an elected plebeian tribune through the authority of the oracle at Delphi (always a patrician). For excerpts of this speech, see Satyanarayana and Tharu (2013, 25-6). Ambedkar's worst fears on the question of representation and final authority became a reality five years after the Mahad events when Gandhi's suicide threat forced him to sign the Poona Pact of 1932. Therefore, in Annihilation of Caste, he returns to the theme of the Conflict of Orders with the bitterness of experience. See also Note 10 on Bodh Gaya in Ambedkar's "A Reply to the Mahatma".

28. Martin Luther (1483-1546), German monk who held the chair of Theology at the University of Wittenberg, was a key figure (along with John Calvin, John Wycliffe and Jan Hus) in the sixteenth-century Reformation movement. He sought to shift the religious leadership's focus away from fees and payments as part of a renewal of the medieval Church. The reformers hoped to restore and clarify the core tenets of the faith, which they would then make accessible to all Christians. For a history of European Reformation, see Peter G. Wallace (2004).

29. The English Civil War (1642—51), which questioned the prerogative of the king and challenged theory of divine right, owed much to the spirit of European Reformation. The Puritans—who espoused a militant, biblically based Calvinistic Protestantism—sought to 'purify' the Church of England of remnants of the Catholic popery, and argued that the Anglican Church established by Queen Elizabeth was far too close to Roman Catholicism. ('Puritan' means that the followers had a pure soul and lived a good life.) Alexis de Tocqueville (1805—59), the French political thinker best known for his two-volume Democracy in America (1835, 1840), argued that the tradition of political liberty in the United States of America began with the

settling of New England by the Puritans from England. For an in-depth study of debates around puritanism and liberty in England, see Puritanism and Liberty, being the Army Debates (1647-9) from the Clarke Manuscripts with Supplementary Documents in A.S.P. Woodhouse (1951). This contains the Putney Debates, the Whitehall Debates, and numerous other documents about Puritan religious and political views during the English Revolution.

30. Prophet Muhammad (570—632 CE) unified scores of warring Arab tribes into a single religious polity (ummah, community) under Islam (which means to submit, surrender). For a concise history of Islam, see Karen Armstrong (2000), who writes: "Muhammad had become the head of a collection of tribal groups that were not bound together by blood but by a shared ideology, an astonishing innovation in Arabian society" (14). Nobody was forced to convert, but all Muslims belonged to one ummah, they could not attack one another, and they vowed to give one another protection.

31. Chandragupta Maurya (340—298 BCE), founder of the Mauryan dynasty, is credited with being t first emperor to rule large parts of the Indian subcontinent as one state. Gautama Buddha (c. 563—483 BCE), on whose teachings Buddhism was founded, preceded him. Chandragupta's grandson was the emperor Ashoka (304-232 BCE), who turned from a warmonger to an advocate of Buddhism and pacifism (though he continued to give the death penalty till the end of his reign).

32. The allusion here is to the Varkari tradition that was established in western India with the Brah Dnyandev or Dnyaneswar, and the Untouchable Cokhamela in the fourteenth century, and was followed by saint-poets from the subaltern castes like Namdeo, Bahinabai and Tukaram into the seventeenth century. While Ambedkar disregarded the piety of Cokhamela, he quite often quoted the radical Tukaram who was Shivaji's contemporary. For a discussion of the political aspects of Tukaram, who was of the Kunabi peasant caste, and his influence on Shivaji, see Gail Omvedt (2008, 109-32). A varkar is a pilgrim, and the Varkari tradition revolves around the god Vithoba or Vitthala in Pandharpur (in Maharashtra's Solapur district). In popular lore Vitthala has come to be regarded as a form of Krishna and this tradition is seen as Vaishnavite. The Varkari cult is seven hundred years old, and with

it begins the Marathi literary tradition, according to Omvedt (85). She discusses how scholars believe Vitthala could have had origins in Saivism, Buddhism or even among pastoral nomadic tribes. Omvedt discusses the Sanskritisation and Vishnu-isation of Vitthala and believes the god could have been originally female ("wide hips, narrow waist, busty, long hair, straight though harsh face") and that contemporary Dalit Buddhists point to "the god's blackness as evidence of indigenous origins" based on iconography (see 85—90). For an overview of the Bhakti tradition and sants in Maharashtra, see Zelliot and Berntsen (1998). Also see the volume edited by Lele (1981).

33. Guru Nanak (1469-1539) was the first of the ten gurus and founder of the Sikh religion. He start a strand of nirguni (without attributes) Bhakti tradition that advocated spending one's life immersed in nam simran (remembrance of the divine name). Guru Nanak and the gurus that followed him preached spiritual equality against varnashrama dharma and imparted their teaching to devotees from all castes. Puri (2003, 2694) writes that while the Sikh holy book, Guru Granth Sahib, includes compositions by Kabir, a weaver, and Ravidas, a tanner (Chamar), the ten gurus of Sikhism came from Khatri families—the highest caste among Sikhs—and married their children within their caste. Despite the preaching of spiritual equality in the eyes of god, there was no expectation on the part of the gurus or their devotees to give up caste identity and thus the doctrine was not translated into social equality.

34. Ambedkar is referring here to the socialists within the Congress who in 1934 formed a faction called the Congress Socialist Party (CSP). Jawaharlal Nehru, at this juncture, was also actively advocating socialist ideas but did join the CSP.

35. Comitia Centuriata, or the Century Assembly, was originally an assembly of the Roman military but soon turned into a political assembly, and became one of the three public assemblies of the Republic of Rome where citizens, grouped into 'centuries', voted on legislative, electoral and judicial matters. In the early days, entry to the Senate was only by birth and rank—so the patricians called the shots. Even in the Comitia Centuriata, instituted in about 450 BCE, entry was restricted initially to the patricians and

the plebeians were kept at bay. Even after the Comitia Centuriata came to include plebeians, its organisation and voting system nevertheless gave greater influence to the rich than to the poor, which as Ambedkar points out, resembled the Communal Award. Ambedkar understands, in the caste context, the plight of plebeians with voting rights as being similar to that of Untouchables who were denied a separate electorate— the mere right to vote does not necessarily empower them. For more on the evolution of the Roman republic, see Olga Tellegen-Couperus (1993).

36. While Delphi, associated with the Greek god Apollo, was an important site in Hellenic politica life, the Romans did not seem to consult the Oracle regularly owing to its considerable distance from Rome. They, however, tended to refer to the Sibylline Books, kept at the Capitolium. See Fontenrose (1978). For an account of the hold of religion on the Romans, see R□pke (2007).

37. Ambedkar's ire here is likely directed at the socialist turn within the Congress. Following the I Congress session in Lucknow, where Nehru took over as party president at Gandhi's behest, the Agrarian Resolution declared that "the most important and urgent problem of the country is the appalling poverty, unemployment and indebtedness of the peasantry, fundamentally due to the antiquated and repressive land revenue system". Nehru and the few socialists he managed to sneak into the thirteen-member Congress Working Committee (CWC)—Acharya Narayan Dev, Jayaprakash Narayan and Achyut Patwardhan—sought to end the 'middle class domination' of the Congress and sought direct representation for peasants and workers in the party. But tacitly backed by Gandhi, the right wing within the Congress opposed Nehru's socialist tendencies. On 29 June 1936, CWC members Babu Rajendra Prasad, Jairamdas Daulatram, Jamnalal Bajaj, Acharya Kripalani and S.D. Dev submitted their resignations from the CWC in a joint letter, contending that Nehru's preaching of socialism in his election speeches was "prejudicial to the interests of the country and to the success of the national struggle for freedom". Gandhi backed the conservatives, as did the business classes. Subsequently Nehru recanted. For a detailed account of Nehru and socialism, see R.C. Dutt (1980, 30-90).

38. Ambedkar (in Das, 2010b, 49—68) mounts a more direct attack on the socialists in the president address delivered on 12 and 13 February 1938 to the GIP (Great Indian Peninsular) Railway Depressed Classes Workmen's Conference held in Nashik, Manmad district. In this speech he offers a trenchant critique of capitalism and Brahminism, and examines the problems with Indian socialists at greater length. Ambedkar was addressing the GIP conference in his capacity as president of the Independent Labour Party, the first political party founded by him in August 1936, a few months after the publication of Annihilation of Caste.
39. Emphasis in original.
40. Ambedkar is echoing the words of Dewey. According to Mukherjee (2009, 347): "So deeply embedded is Dewey's thought in Ambedkar's consciousness that quite often his words flow through Ambedkar's discourse without quotation marks." She also notes "how Ambedkar culled sentences from Democracy and Education to describe his version of the ideal society" (351). Ambedkar expresses his debt to Dewey in section 25.4 of AoC. The relevant paragraph from Dewey's Democracy and Education, quoted by Mukherjee, reads: "A democratic criterion requires us to develop capacity to the point of competency to choose and make its own career. This principle is violated when the attempt is made to fit individuals in advance for definite industrial callings, selected not on the basis of trained original capacities, but on that of the wealth or social status of parents" (364). See Dewey (1916). All further citations from Democracy and Education are from the online edition.
41. John Dewey was an advocate of industrial democracy, which, in Noam Chomsky's (2003) wor "means democratising production, commerce, and so on, which means eliminating the whole structure of capitalist hierarchy". Chomsky terms Dewey a "radical" in this interview. In another essay, Chomsky (2013) says: "Dewey called for workers to be 'masters of their own industrial fate' and for all institutions to be brought under public control, including the means of production, exchange, publicity, transportation and communication. Short of this, Dewey argued, politics will remain 'the shadow cast on society by big business.'"
42. This latter sentence also echoes Dewey (1916): "Sentimentally, it may seem harsh to say that th greatest evil of the present regime

is not found in poverty and in the suffering which it entails, but in the fact that so many persons have callings which make no appeal to them, which are pursued simply for the money reward that accrues. For such callings constantly provoke one to aversion, ill will, and a desire to slight and evade" (cited in Mukherjee 2009, 364).

43. Ethnology draws upon ethnographic material to compare and contrast different cultures. Ethnography is the study of single groups through direct contact with their cultures. In the nineteenth century, ethnologists and ethnographers studied caste mainly as a subsidiary exercise in the supposedly higher and grander task of uncovering the evolutionary heritage of all humanity. In doing so they contributed to the 'Orientalist' exercise of the census and gazetteers and to the racial understanding of caste. Caste was thus subsumed into theories of biologically determined race essences. Ambedkar, in fact, begins his 1916 essay, "Castes in India", with a reference to ethnology. Further, on caste and ethnology, see Bayly (1999, 11-19); and Dirks (2001,126—38). See also Ketkar (1909/1998, 165-70).

44. Devadatta Ramakrishna Bhandarkar (1875—1950) was an epigraphist and archaeologist who worked for the Archaeological Survey of India. Ambedkar is citing from p.37 of this 1911 essay. Based on epigraphic research, Bhandarkar uses evidence from the Vedas and the epics of the Hindu tradition, such as the Rig Veda and the Mahabharata, to disprove the 'purity of blood' myth attributed to Brahmins. "It may be said that after all the Mahabharata ... is a conglomeration of legends, which are not of much historical importance, though they cannot be objected to by an orthodox Brahmana and consequently may be adduced to silence his pretensions to purity of origin and the consequent highest place in Hindu society" (1911, 10).

45. In his understanding of the caste system and its evolution, Ambedkar here differs strongly from Brahminic appropriations (such as by B.G. Tilak who authored The Arctic Home in the Vedas, 1903) of the racial theory of Aryans and Dravidians propounded by European Indologists. In fact, as seen in Roy's introduction to this edition, even Gandhi, in his South Africa years, strongly believed in the British and India's ruling classes

both being 'Aryan'. Ambedkar, however, also differs on this front from his predecessor and radical thinker Jotiba Phule and his contemporary fellow-traveller 'Periyar' E.V. Ramasamy Naicker (1879—1973) who turned the racial theory inside out, postulated a pre-Aryan golden age, and regarded the Brahmins as Aryans, and hence foreigners, who imposed the caste system upon the non-Brahmins who were seen as an indigenous race. For Phule's writings, especially Gulamgiri (Slavery, 1873), see G.P. Deshpande (2002, 23-101). Perivar, on the eve of independence, quite radically called upon the Dravidian people of South India to "guard against the transfer of power from the British to the Aryans" (The Hindu, 11 February 1946). As sociologist T.K. Oommen (2005, 99) argues, "According to Periyar, Brahmins had tried to foist their language and social system on Dravidians to erase their race consciousness and, therefore, he constantly reminded the Dravidians to uphold their 'race consciousness'. However, Periyar did not advocate the superiority of one race over the other but insisted on [the] equality of all races. Thus the fundamental difference between Aryan Hinduism and Dravidian Hinduism is crucial: the former [is] hegemonic, but the latter is emancipatory."

46. Eugenics is the 'science' of predicting and controlling heredity that was popular at the turn of th twentieth century, in that it was perceived to be an effort at the 'improvement' of the human species. The term was coined by Francis Galton inspired by Darwin's theory of natural selection as well as the rediscovery of Mendel's work on heredity (see also Note 47). Galton advocated that only the best and most meritorious should be encouraged to breed; a more disastrous strand of his theory led to Hitler's 'final solution'. According to Mark Singleton (2007, 125—46), the popularity of eugenics in India can be understood by the place it occupied as a 'scientific explanation' for the 'degeneration' of Hindu society and colonial subjugation by the British. Another reason for the popularity of eugenics was its valorisation of the endogamy of the caste system as a mechanism of racial purity.

47. For a good example of the use of eugenics to defend caste, see TN. Roy (1927, 67—72), who begins with this assertion: "The greatest eugenic movement that the world has as yet witnessed originated in India. It was the institution of the caste system." Arguing that

"the earliest eugenic movement began with the institution of what is known as Gotra", Roy blames the "downfall of Hinduism" on not observing caste distinctions well enough. "The Brahmin was originally created by eugenic selection," he argues, and gives the finest examples of intellect in Bengal as being all Brahmin men—Raja Ram Mohan Roy, Ishwar Chandra Vidyasagar and Bankim Chandra Chatterjee.

48. William Bateson (1861—1926) was a British scientist and is considered the founder of genetics. wrote Mendel's Principles of Heredity (1909) after the discovery of Gregor Mendel's article written in 1866. Ambedkar is citing from p.205 of Bateson's book. Bateson elaborated his own research findings following the investigation of Mendel's theories. This discovery laid down the basis for not only genetics but also eugenics. However, early into his research Bateson had recognised the dangers of the application of genetics to social engineering and warned against the uniformising tendencies of eugenic thinking. See Harvey (1995).

49. Ambedkar here slips into an essentialist understanding of caste, race and morphology. He is drawing upon a British military categorisation of working class soldiers during the First World War. Then British Prime Minister David Lloyd George lamented: "How can Britain run an Al empire with a C3 population?" Ina Zweiniger-Bargielowska (2006) argues that though the obsession with a deteriorating national health and physical fitness echoed fascist narratives, these eugenic categories were used as metaphors across the poEtical spectrum in Britain. Ambedkar is using this premise to dismiss the 'biological' defence of the caste system. See also the work of Heather Streets (2004), who discusses how the British, from 1857 to 1914, identified and taxonomised 'martial races' that are believed to possess a biological or cultural disposition to the racial and masculine qualities necessary for the arts of war.

50. In AoC 1936 and subsequent editions, this reads as: "Caste cannot and has not improved race."

51. Derived from Sindhu, the native name for the Indus river, the term Hind was first used in Persia and came to be established after the eleventh-century polymath Al-Biruni (973—1048), commissioned by the king Mahmud of Ghazni (in present-day Afghanistan),

travelled to the Indian subcontinent in 1017 and wrote the famous encyclopedic account of India called Tarikh al-Hind. The word 'Hindu', derived thus, did not indicate a religious group but was used as a geographical demarcator for the inhabitants of the land near and east of the Indus. Later, the word may have been adopted by those inhabitants to distinguish themselves from the Muslims who came to initially rule the northern parts of India. The ancient texts that so-called Hindus today claim their roots from—the Vedas, Ramayana, Mahabharata, Bhagvad Gita, Upanishads—do not ever use the terms Hindu or Hindusim. Recent research argues that the terms came into vogue with Orientalist and colonial scholarship. For an overview of the debates around 'Hindu' and 'Hinduism' and a nuanced counter-argument see D.N. Lorenzen (2006, 7—10). See also Romila Thapar's essay, "Syndicated Hinduism" (1989/2001, 54) where she says, "The term Hinduism as we understand it today to describe a particular religion is modern." Ambedkar, for his times, was farsighted in jettisoning a term around which Indian nationalism and anticolonialism came to be constructed.

52. The phrase 'consciousness of kind' was coined by the American sociologist Franklin Henry Giddings (1855—1931), and was first elaborated in The Principles of Sociology (1896). Giddings sought to define the fundamental underlying law that defined human society. He defined 'consciousness of kind' as "a state of consciousness in which any being, whether low or high in the scale of life, recognises another conscious being as of like kind with itself." See Giddings (1896/2004, 17).
53. Rendered as "communion" in AoC 1936 and subsequent editions.
54. This echoes Dewey's words in Democracy and Education (1916): "Society exists not only by transmission, by communication, but it may fairly be said to exist in transmission, in communication."
55. The Sahyadrikhand is a latter-day addition to the Skanda Purana, the most volatile of Sanskrit texts, continuously expanding and incorporating new traditions. Wendy Doniger (1993, 60) terms it "surely the shiftiest, or sandiest, of all" puranas (collections of stories revolving around divinities and myths that allude to history though they cannot be accused of historicity). The Sahyadrikhand recounts the genealogy of several Maharashtrian Brahmin sub-castes to incorporate them into caste hierarchy. See also Rao (2009, 55).

Ambedkar (BAWS 3, 48) elsewhere writes of the Sahyadrikhand: "It assigns noble origin to other castes while it assigns to the Brahmin caste the filthiest origin. It was a revenge on Manu. It was the worst lampoon on the Brahmins as a caste. The Peshwas very naturally ordered its destruction. Some survived the general destruction."

56. Golak or Govardhan Brahmins are a sub-caste in western India (largely Maharashtra) considere of inferior birth by other Brahmin communities of the region. See Hassan (1920). Deorukha (Devrukhe) Brahmins and Karada (Karhade) are sub-castes of the Panchadravid (living south of the Vindhya mountains) Maharashtrian Brahmins. Palshe is another Maharashtrian Brahmin sub-caste considered inferior by Chitpavan Brahmins. In Anandrav Bhikaji Phadke vs. Shankar Daji Charye (1883 1LR 7 Bom 323) the Bombay Court upheld the right of Chitpavan Brahmins to exclude Palshe Brahmins from worshipping at a temple, on the ground that such an exclusive right is one which the courts must guard, as otherwise all 'high-caste Hindus' would hold their sanctuaries and perform their worship only so far as those of the 'lower castes' chose to allow them (Naval 2004, 14).

57. The origin of the Chitpavan Brahmins is traced to the myth of Parashurama, believed to be an 'immortal' Brahmin incarnation of Vishnu. Parashurama is said to have burned the bodies of fourteen people who were washed ashore on a funeral pyre, purifying them, and then restored them to life— thus the name chita (pyre) pavan (purified). These fourteen people are said to be of Jewish, Persian or, in some versions, Berber descent. Another version gives the etymology of their name as "pure of the mind" (Figueira 2002, 121-33). Their recorded history, however, begins in the eighteenth century, when Chattrapati Shahu, grandson of Shivaji, appointed Balaji Vishwanath Bhat, a Chitpavan Brahmin, as Peshwa (Johnson 2005, 58). M.G. Ranade, founder- member of the Indian National Congress; G.K. Gokhale, 'moderate' Congress leader and mentor to M.K. Gandhi; Pandita Ramabai, a pioneer of education and women's rights; B.G Tilak, Hindu nationalist leader; Vinoba Bhave, 'spiritual successor' to Gandhi; V.D. Savarkar, who coined the term Hindutva, and who was one of the co-accused in Gandhi's assassination; and Nathuram Godse, who assassinated Gandhi, were all Chitpavan Brahmins.

58. The Wars of the Roses were fought between 1455 and 1485 between Lancaster and York, two houses of the royal line Plantagenet. Ambedkar most probably is referring to the Second English Civil War as the Cromwellian war which was fought between the parliamentarians and the royalists in 1648— 59, in which Cromwell and his parliamentarian forces defeated the royalists and established the precedent that the king can only rule with the Parliament's consent.
59. In 1674, the Deccan Brahmins refused to allow the coronation of Shivaji, the Maratha king (1627/30—80), according to Vedic rites. They doubted his Kshatriya origins and saw him as a Shudra claimant. As Rao (2009, 42) says: "A Brahmin from Benares, Gaga Bhatta, supported Shivaji's claim to Kshatriya status after much persuasion and traced the Bhosle lineage to the Sisodia Rajputs of Udaipur." Gaga Bhatta is also said to have charged a hefty fee for legitimising Shivaji's claim. On Shivaji's coronation story, see V.S. Bendrey (1960); see also Laine (2003), a book that was banned in Maharashtra in 2004. (The ban was lifted in 2007 by the Bombay High Court and this was upheld by the Supreme Court of India in 2010.) A recent paper by Rosalind O'Hanlon (2010a) throws light on the migration of several Maratha Brahmins to Benares in the sixteenth century and the story behind Gaga Bhatta's return to the Konkan region in the mid-seventeenth century.
60. Kayasthas are a caste of scribes whose varna status has been the subject of a raging debate. Wh they trace their origin to Chitragupta, the scribe of god Yama, and claim a status equal to Brahmins, or to Kshatriyas, many Brahmin texts position them as Shudras. The poet (and Kayastha) Harivansh Rai Bachchan (1998, 7) writes that Brahmins "have sought to degrade the Kayasthas in many a Sanskrit verse such as the following: That the foetal Kayastha eats not his mother's flesh/ speaks not of tenderness, but of toothlessness." The Peshwa Brahmins of the Deccan had resented the Kayasthas' right to learning and becoming scribes and record-keepers in the seventeenth century. "The head of the state, though a Brahman, was despised by his other Brahman servants, because the first Peshwa's great-grandfather's great-grandfather had once been lower in society than the Desh Brahmans' great-grandfathers' great-grandfathers. While the Chitpavan Brahmans

were waging social war with the Deshastha Brahmans, a bitter jealousy raged between the Brahman ministers and governors and the Kayastha secretaries" (Sarkar 1948, 357). See also Sections 9.1- 3 of AoC. Further, see O'Hanlon (2010b) who says from the mid-fifteenth century, periodic but intense disputes developed over Kayastha entitlement to the rituals of the twice-born. "Often migrants who had come into the Maratha regions as servants of the Bahmani kings and to Deccan Sultanate states, Kayasthas were intruders into local societies whose Brahmin communities had hitherto commanded more exclusive possession of scribal skills" (566). See also Note 108 at 18.1.

61. In AoC 1936 and 1937, Ambedkar uses "excluded and partially excluded areas"; whereas the 1 edition uses "excluded and partially included areas". Since the latter is incorrect, the former has been retained.

62. Ambedkar is referring to the constitutional discussions culminating in the Government of India of 1935 in which areas inhabited by tribals were classified as "excluded" and "partially excluded areas" for the purpose of administration. Laws were only applicable in these areas when the governor approved it, purportedly not to harm these "backward" societies with the implementation of laws instituted for the more "developed" parts of India. See also Chandra (2013).

63. Ambedkar is referring to the Government of India Act of 1935 as the new Constitution.

64. Ambedkar's views on Adivasis—officially classified as Scheduled Tribes—are problematic. Even as he appears well intentioned and protectionist, he argues for "civilising the savages" and looks at them as leading the life of "hereditary animals", and even warns "the Hindus" that the "aborigines are a source of potential danger". Later, in his address to the All-India Scheduled Castes Federation held in Bombay on 6 May 1945, ("The Communal Deadlock and a Way to Solve It"), while discussing the issue of proportionate representation, he says: "My proposals do not cover the Aboriginal Tribes although they are larger in number than the Sikhs, Anglo-Indians, Indian Christians and Parsees ... [T]he Aboriginal Tribes have not as yet developed any political sense to make the best use of their political opportunities and they may easily become mere

instruments in the hands either of a majority or a minority and thereby disturb the balance without doing any good to themselves ... the proper thing to do for these backward communities is to establish a Statutory Commission to administer what are now called the 'excluded areas' on the same basis as was done in the case of the South African Constitution. Every Province in which these excluded areas are situated should be compelled to make an annual contribution of a prescribed amount for the administration of these areas" (BAWS 1, 375, emphasis added). Ironically, Gandhi used a similar logic to argue that the Untouchables had not yet developed the political sense to use the vote, let alone make use of separate electorates that Ambedkar had championed and won for the Untouchables in the 1931 Round Table Conferences. Shashank Kela (2012, 297—8) says, "Racism and prejudice marked the Constituent Assembly's 'adivasi' debates. Members referred to their subhuman existence, primitiveness and propensity for summary justice; invoked the threat of separatism; and adduced arguments of the greatest good of the greatest numbers." Uday Chandra (2013) has argued how both Ambedkar and Jawaharlal Nehru partook of a liberalist-colonial understanding, and fear, of the 'primitive' during the making of the Constitution of independent India, almost retaining the colonialist approach to so-called tribals. In contrast, the Adivasi leader from Jharkhand and member of the Constitutent Assembly (CA), Jaipal Singh, had argued on 19 December 1946: "What my people require, Sir, is not adequate safeguards ... We do not ask for any special protection. We want to be treated like every other Indian." As Chandra points out, this was a perception shared by Vallabhbhai Patel, Chairman of the Tribal and Excluded Areas Committee and future Home Minister. However, later, during the CA debates on the Sixth Schedule, the Ambedkar-led proposal to allow Scheduled Tribes to function from excluded areas found favour with Adivasi spokespersons such as Rev. J.J.M. Nichols- Roy, who said on 19 November 1949: "The Sixth Schedule concerns the hill-districts of Assam in which the hill men in Assam live by themselves in their own territories, who have their own language and their culture and the Constituent Assembly has rightly agreed ... that there should be councils for these different districts in order to enable the people who live in those areas to develop themselves according to their genius and culture." For the workings of autonomous district councils established under the Sixth Schedule in the Northeastern states, see Bengt G. Karlsson (2011) and Sanjib Baruah (2007).

65. By the beginning of the twentieth century, huge sections of the population, mostly itinerant, were labelled criminal under the Criminal Tribes Acts of 1871 and 1911. Seeing criminality as hereditary was a logical outcome of the caste system. If people could be born scholars, weavers and cobblers they could also be born thieves and thugs. See D'Souza (2001) and Radhakrishna (2001).

66. Anaryas: Sanskrit for non-Aryans. Anasa (literally those without a nose, figuratively those with an aquiline nose) is another term frequently used in the Vedas to refer to the local, indigenous populations, whom the Aryas regarded as different from them and therefore to be stigmatised.

67. Pathare means stone and prabhu means lord. This caste claims to have descended from the Kshatriyas. The mythological claim around origins goes thus: "The first of them was Ashvapati (700 BCE), a lineal descendant of Rama and Prithu, who, as is stated in the local chronology, governed India in the Dvapara and Treta Yugas, which is a good while ago! The Patarah Prabhus are the only caste within which Brahmans have to perform certain purely Vedic rites known under the name of the 'Kshatriya rites'" (Blavatsky, 1892/2010, 145—6). Veena Naregal (2001, 168—9) says: "In western India it was mainly brahmins and some sub-brahmin groups like the prabhus and shenvis who were among the first to perceive the benefits of the new literate order and respond to the opportunities it created. The prabhus and the shenvis were traditionally trained scribes who had a long and successful history of employment as karkuns in different parts of the Peshwa kingdom and in the offices of the colonial trading houses of Bombay. The possession of uncommon literate skills had also allowed the prabhus to be closely associated with pre-modern book production." See also Uma Chakravarti (2000) for a discussion of the Peshwa intervention on norms for widows and enforced widowhood claims of upwardly mobile middle caste groups.

68. On Daivadnya (also Daivajna) Brahmins, the Census of India (1961, 14) says: "They are locall known as 'Sonars' and 'Sonagars' and are the traditional goldsmiths. They are found in almost all the

towns and big villages of North Kanara District. They are said to have migrated from Goa."

69. Here Ambedkar is referring to the polemics used by the Vedic missionaries of the Arya Samaj t counter the influence of Muslim and Christian preachers and missionaries— adopting their established practices of preaching at religious fairs, challenging missionaries in pamphlets and on the streets. The rise of the Arya Samaj owed much to the demographic shifts that characterised the history of the Punjab due to its proximity to Central Asia and the predominance of Sikh and Muslim rulers. In the nineteenth century, British rule added to this list, and the conversions of the oppressed castes in large numbers to Islam and Christianity exacerbated the situation. See Jones (2006, 139-45). According to Gopal Krishan (2004, 77-89), in 1881, the Hindus constituted 43.8 per cent of the population, the Sikhs 8.2 per cent and Christians 0.1 per cent. The Muslims, at 47.6 per cent, were well short of an absolute majority. But by 1941, the Muslims were in absolute majority in the Punjab accounting for 53.2 per cent of the total population. The Hindus made 29.1 per cent of the total, the Sikhs 14.9 per cent, Christians 1.9 per cent and others 1.3 per cent. The erosion in the percentage share of the Hindus was caused by the conversion of many Hindus—especially the 'lower castes', such as Chuhras, Chamars, Jhiwars and Malis—to Islam, Sikhism and Christianity.
70. Reads in AoC 1936 as: "Whether the Hindu religion is a missionary religion is a question whicH was once a subject of controversy." Amended in 1937.
71. For a discussion of conversion during the colonial period, see Gauri Viswanathan (1998), especially the chapter "Conversion to Equality" (211—40) that discusses Ambedkar's quest for equality through conversion. Also see Chakravarti (2000), where she alludes to the problems of the convert, Pandita Ramabai, in terms of cultural and 'nationalist' positions vis-a-vis the colonial structure which bear out Ambedkar's point.
72. Phrase added in AoC 1937.
73. Shuddhi or shuddhikaran—a movement for 'reconversion' to Hinduism—was initiated by Dayananda Saraswati, founder of the Arya Samaj. In 1877, two years after founding the Arya Samaj, Dayananda is said to have performed the first ever shuddhi of a

Muslim man (Parel 2000, 122). Swami Shraddhananda (1856—1926) carried on this legacy more militantly in the early twentieth century in the Punjab and the United Provinces. For an account, see Jaffrelot (1995). However, as Ambedkar points out, shuddhi created many problems since the privileged castes were not willing to mingle with newly 'purified' lower caste members. See also Jones (2006, 129-35, 202-14).

74. The Hindu Mahasabha launched the sangathan movement in the early 1920s in response to the Khilafat Movement (1918—24), which had Gandhi's support, aimed at a pan-Islamic mobilisation to save the Ottoman Empire from dismemberment and to secure political reforms for India. The underlying logic of sangathan was to defend the Hindu community from so-called foreign forces through organisation and unification. It aimed to integrate the different sections of the Hindu community, including the Untouchables. The main proponents of sangathan were Bhai Parmanand (see Note 11 in Prologue) and V.D. Savarkar. See Jaffrelot (1999a, 19—24) and also Bapu (2013, 47-60).
75. Ambedkar is invoking the Deweyan concept of "associated life", which he picks up and develo further into a political tool. Both Dewey and Ambedkar believed that democracy should not be restricted to the political realm, but should also manifest itself in other areas, such as education, industry and the public sphere. See Mukherjee (2009, 356).
76. A feeling of brotherhood (ikhwaan) among Muslims across the world (ummat) is an important conceptual category in Islam. Sikhs are also enjoined by their religion to practise universal brotherhood and often address each other as bhai (brother).
77. Sava lakh: 125,000. The complete phrase, "Sava lakh se ek laraun" (My one follower will tak on 125,000), is attributed to Govind Singh, the tenth Sikh Guru, who is said to have given this battle cry at Chamkaur in 1704.
78. William Morris (1834-96) was a poet, author, leader of the early British socialist movement, a the founder of the Arts and Crafts Movement in Britain. The quote is from A Dream of John Ball (1888), a dream travel in time to the Peasants' Revolt of 1381 (also known as Wat Tyler's Rebellion or the Great Rising). Ambedkar here is quoting from the speech given by the character of John Ball, a radical

travelling priest excommunicated for his preaching of equality to the Kentish rebels.

79. Endosmosis was another Deweyan term that Ambedkar deployed and developed. It is derived f a biological term which means the passage of a fluid through a permeable membrane from a region of lower to a region of higher concentration. Mukherjee points out that the term was used originally by the French philosopher Henri Louis Bergson (1859-1941) and, after him, by American philosopher and psychologist William James (1842—1910), who was, like Dewey, a leading exponent of pragmatism, "to describe the interaction of the mind with nature". Dewey appropriated it as a descriptor for interaction between social groups. In Ambedkar and Dewey's work the term came to be a metaphor of the fluidity of communications between social groups, in which, according to Mukherjee (2009, 352), they managed to reconcile the two extremes and give a sense of being both separate and connected.
80. These lines appear almost exactly in Dewey's Democracy and Education, chapter 7: "A democracy is more than a form of government; it is primarily a mode of associated living, of conjoint communicated experience."
81. In AoC 1936 this part reads as: "men were treated unequally unequally as they are"; in 1937 as: "men were treated unequally as they are". The 1945 version is retained here.
82. It must be remembered that the Jat-Pat Todak Mandal, which invited Ambedkar for its annual conference, for which this address was prepared, was originally affiliated to the Arya Samaj and continued to have several important Arya Samaj leaders of the Punjab influencing it. Ambedkar chooses to take them on in this section of his speech, and this would likely have made them most uncomfortable, and caused them to withdraw their invitation to him. For a summary of the Arya Samaj's views on varnashrama (also known as chaturvarnya and varnavyavastha), based on Dayananda Saraswati's 'Vedic' approach, see Jones (2006).
83. Refer to Note 161 at 24.3 on the guna—karma theory.
84. "Savants" in 1936 and 1937; amended in 1944.
85. Text in semibold in this paragraph does not appear in AoC 1936. In the first edition, the lines af the highlighted text appear thus: "It

is human experience that notions and sentiments associated with certain names become part of ourselves, stiffening into attitudes that which hold even trained minds in bondage. Intellectual servitude to old associations is very common and is more difficult to break than is generally thought. Facts may change, but if names remain the same, then the notions associated with those names linger not only in sentiments but also in practice. These labels have had all along in Indian history the de facto connotation of designating a hierarchy of castes based on birth. They were understood to be marks of superiority and inferiority." These lines were amended in the 1937 edition used here.

86. All of this paragraph, except its last sentence, does not appear in AoC 1936.
87. The lines at the beginning of 16.1 till "... a miserable failure" figure under Section XV of AoC 1936. The lines that follow from here (beginning, "From a practical ...") till the first sentence of 16.3 (ending, "... chaturvarnya a success.") have been added in the 1937 edition.
88. This is given as "varna" in AoC 1936 and 1937; Ambedkar changes it to "chaturvarnya" in 194
89. In AoC 1936, Section 16 begins here, with the sentence: "The practicability of the chaturvarnya presupposes two things. It presupposes ..."
90. This question does not appear in AoC 1936.
91. Phrase added in 1937.
92. Plato's The Republic, addressing the question of justice, deduces that the human soul has three parts: the "logical", thinking part; the "spirited" part, by which we develop anger and get into a temper; and the "appetitive" part, by which we experience hunger, thirst, eroticism, love for moneymaking and other such desires. The book also categorises men into three classes based on which part of their soul masks the others: the 'guardians' are persons in whom the logical part dominates, in the 'auxiliaries' spirit dominates, and the 'producers' are people who have let their appetite dominate. The guardians must rule, the auxiliaries must help in running the guardians' writ, and the producers must work. (See also Note 161 on the guna—karma theory.) Ambedkar disagrees with Plato on many levels. He is not convinced that there are only three qualities on the basis of which a soul can be divided. He believes that the multitude of human characteristics is so complex that it

is impossible to identify and categorise them. He also points out that different characteristics become more or less important in the same person at different times. His criticism is also what was later popularised as the problem of the 'one- dimensional man' by Herbert Marcuse (1964/1991). From his experience of caste, Ambedkar's critique is that in such an arrangement where most of the power is vested with the guardians and the remaining with the auxiliaries (the 'twice-born' Brahmins, Kshatriyas and Vaishyas in the caste context), there is no mechanism to ensure that they will not oppress the producers (Shudras and Untouchables).

93. In AoC 1936, this merely reads as "not possible to pigeon men into holes". In 1937, Ambedkar amends this to "not possible to pigeon men into holes according as he belongs to one class or the other". The subsequent lines, beginning "That it is impossible ..." till "... it was established?" in 16.6 are absent in AoC 1936.
94. This sentence begins with "Another" in AoC 1936; perhaps changed in the light of new sentence added in 1937.
95. The word used is "existence" in AoC 1936.
96. The story of Shambuka is told in the seventh book, Uttarakanda, of the Valmiki Ramayana. Shambuka wants to achieve a higher status than the suras (devtas, gods) through meditation and austerities. On discovering that Shambuka, a Shudra, was indeed meditating, Rama promptly beheads him to restore varnasharma dharma. The story has been used by the Dravidian movement and in anticaste literature to ridicule the idea of Rama as the embodiment of perfection. Kuvempu (Kuppalli Venkatappa Puttappa) (1904—94), a Jnanpith-winning Kannada author wrote Sudra Tapasvi (1944), a novel based on Shambuka's life. Sikhamani, a contemporary Telugu Dalit poet, writes: "The sword that severed/ Shambuka's head could remain/ sharp and safe for centuries./ It has just changed hands/and no longer recognises you./ No Manu to save you now!" See "Steel Nibs are Sprouting ..." in Satyanarayana and Tharu (2013, 554).
97. The Manusmriti represents itself as the dharma that Brahma declares to Manu, 'the first Man', a is passed on by him to Bhrigu, one of the ten 'great sages'. The text is believed to have attained its present form around the second century CE. Ambedkar writes in another, posthumously published work, Revolution and Counter-

Revolution in Ancient India (BAWS 5, 273): "Pushvamitra Sunga and his successors could not have tolerated these exaggerated claims of the Brahmins unless they themselves were Brahmins interested in the establishment of Brahmanism. Indeed it is quite possible that the Manusmriti was composed at the command of Pushvamitra Brahman king (185—149 BC) himself, and forms the book of the philosophy of Brahmanism." In another work, The Untouchables: Who Were They and Why they Became Untouchable, Ambedkar (BAWS 9, 373) says: "After taking all facts into consideration Prof B□hler has fixed a date which appears to strike the truth. According to B□hler, the Manusmriti, in the shape in which it exists now, came into existence in the Second Century AD." A contemporary scholar, J.L. Brockington (1996, 92) arrives at a similar conclusion. Many editions of the Manusmriti have been published in Sanskrit since its first edition in 1813. The first translation was Institutes of Hindu law, or, The ordinances of Menu [sic], according to the gloss of Culluca: comprising the Indian system of duties, religious and civil: verbally translated from the original Sanscrit: with a preface , by Sir William Jones (1796). One of the best-known translations is George Buhler's Laws of Manu (1886/2004), which contains an exhaustive introduction and extracts from seven commentaries. In her modern translation, Wendy Doniger states that no work in the tradition of Western scholarship compares with the fame and sustained authority exercised across centuries by the Manusmriti. See Doniger and Smith (1991, xviii-xix). As C.J. Fuller (2003, 484) notes, British administrators depended on Dharmashastras such as the Manusmriti to develop a legal system for India, thus subjecting the Hindu population as a whole to a Brahminical legal code. For the most authoritative, exhaustively annotated edition (1,131 pages) of the Manusmriti, see Patrick Olivelle (2005).

98. Such verses do not figure in the Manusmriti. B□hler's edition, which Ambedkar may have poss accessed, offers two verses that come close to the import. "A once-born man (a Shudra), who insults a twice-born man with gross invective, shall have his tongue cut out; for he is of low origin" (8.270; 1886/2004, 211). And: "If he arrogantly teaches Brahmins their duty, the king shall cause hot oil

to be poured into his mouth and into his ears" (8.272; 2004, 211). For Ambedkar's extended discussion of the Manusmriti, see the annotated edition of "Castes in India" in Rege (2013, 77—108). Ambedkar seems to be citing these punishments from chapter 12 of Gautama Dharma Sutra (600 BCE to 300 BCE, predating the Manusmriti) which he also cites in his posthumous work, Philosophy of Hinduism (BAWS 3). Buhler's translation (1898, 239) of Gautama Dharma Sutra talks of similar punishments for the Shudra: "4. Now if a Shudra listens intentionally to (a recitation of) the Veda, his ears shall be filled with (molten) tin or lac. 5. If he recites (Vedic texts), his tongue shall be cut out. 6. If he remembers them, his body shall be split in twain. 7. If he assumes a position equal (to that of twice-born men) in sitting, in lying down, in conversation or on the road, he shall undergo (corporal) punishment."

99. Paragraphs 16.8 and 16.9 were added in 1937. The sentence with which 16.9 ends—"Given the difficulties... chaturvarnya."—figures in 1936 as the last sentence of AoC 1936; the word "conditions" is used in the place of "difficulties".

100. In AoC 1936, after "serve", it reads "—all this sounds very simple and appears to be perfect. B what does it all come to in practice? It means the pauperisation of the many for the sake of the few. It means the disarming of the many for the sake of the few. It means the deadening and darkening of the lives of the many in order that the few may have life and light. As has been observed, there is no country in the world which has suffered so much as a result of social evils of its own creation as India." Ambedkar drops this passage in AoC 1937, and in its place offers an extended reflection—of 650 words—on the exploitative and illogical nature of the chaturvarnya system. This appears to be triggered by Gandhi's response to this speech-essay in Harijan, where he upholds the fourfold varnashrama dharma but denounces the proliferation of castes. In this edition, this new material appears from this point in 17.1 till the close of 17.4.

101. Tryavarnikas: Sanskrit for 'three varnas'; refers to the dwija, 'twice-born', varnas.

102. Highlighted words read in AoC 1936 as "similar" (for social), "occurred to" (troubled), "have been able to" (can), and "masses" (lower classes) respectively.

103. 'Direct action' is a method Ambedkar (BASWS 5, 375) advocated for the assertion of the civil rights of Untouchables. When Ambedkar was at Columbia University (1913—16), he was likely exposed to the views of American feminist anarchist Voltairine de Cleyre (1866—1912), whom the anarchist Emma Goldman called the "most gifted and brilliant anarchist woman America ever produced". In 1912, de Cleyre wrote a famous essay called "Direct Action", which she defined as collective action against and mass resistance to state and capitalist oppression. "Every person who ever had a plan to do anything, and went and did it, or who laid his plan before others, and won their cooperation to do it with him, without going to external authorities to please do the thing for them, was a direct actionist ... Every person who ever in his life had a difference with anyone to settle, and went straight to the other persons involved to settle it, either by a peaceable plan or otherwise, was a direct actionist." The term was also popularised by the Industrial Workers of the World founded in 1905 in Chicago; its mouthpiece was called Direct Action. On his part, Ambedkar called for "open revolt in the form of direct action against the Hindu Established Order". He lists the Chavadar Tank satyagraha in Mahad and the Kalaram temple satyagraha as instances of direct action which created a 'crisis' among Hindus. Ambedkar contrasts this method with that of Gandhi's Harijan Sevak Sangh that believed caste Hindus must feel remorse and guilt (for practising untouchability) and thus voluntarily ask the Untouchables to participate in the general village life, that is, accessing waterbodies, roads or temples. Ambedkar here cites his letter to A.V. Thakkar, general secretary of the Harijan Sevak Sangh: "The salvation of the Depressed Classes will come only when the Caste Hindu is made to think and is forced to feel that he must alter his ways. For that you must create a crisis by direct action against his customary code of conduct. The crisis will compel him to think and once he begins to think he will be more ready to change than he is otherwise likely to be. The great defect in the policy of least resistance and silent infiltration of rational ideas lies in that they do not 'compel', for they do not produce a crisis. The direct action in respect of the Chavadar Tank in Mahad 1927, the Kalaram temple in Nasik 1930 and the Guruvayur temple in Malabar 1931-32 have done in a few

days what million days of preaching by reformers would never have done." In the 1920s, Ambedkar did invest a little faith in the Gandhian satyagraha method; as noted in Roy's introduction (p. 107), Gandhi's portrait was displayed during the December leg of the Mahad satyagraha in 1927. Muhammad Ali Jinnah, founder of the All-India Muslim League, also called for 'direct action' in 1946 if the Muslims were not granted Pakistan. For a discussion of Jinnah's lack of clarity on what he meant by direct action, see Ayesha Jalal (1985, 211-3).

104. In AoC 1936, it is the "wretched system of chaturvarnya". Ambedkar in the next few passages o Section 17 consistently replaces references to chaturvarnya with "caste system"—all these instances are highlighted with semibold text.

105. In AoC 1936, this sentence ends with "the fate of eternal servitude".

106. This paragraph does not appear in AoC 1936.

107. The Mauryan empire lasted from 322 BCE to 185 BCE and reached its zenith under Ashoka, wh after securing the empire and extending its borders, embraced Buddhism and spread it through the territories under his control. He even sent ambassadors across Asia to spread the faith. Ambedkar (BAWS 3, 268) considered this Buddhist phase a 'revolution' in ancient India, and termed the re-emergence of Brahminism under the Brahmin king Pushyamitra Sunga (185—149 BCE) the 'counter-revolution': "The Brahmins had not only lost state patronage but they lost their occupation which mainly consisted of performing sacrifices for a fee which oftentimes was very substantial and which constituted their chief source of living. The Brahmins therefore lived as the suppressed and Depressed Classes for nearly 140 years during which the Maurya Empire lasted. A rebellion against the Buddhist state was the only way of escape left to the suffering Brahmins and there is special reason why Pushyamitra should raise the banner of revolt against the rule of the Mauryas."

108. Ambedkar discusses the many conflicts between Brahmins and Kshatriyas at length elsewhere (BAWS 3, 392— 415). Here, he is alluding to the mythical Brahmin warrior Parashurama's twenty-one wars of extermination against the Kshatriyas after Parashurama's father is killed by a Kshatriya and he sees his mother beating her chest twenty-one times. Mythical and legendary

narratives asserting the authority of the Brahmins were in conflict with each other as Brahmin subcastes tried to establish superiority over one another through competitive myth-making. See Figueira (2002). For a typical example of a legalistic inter-Brahmin conflict in modern India, see Notes 56-7 at 7.2. See Johnson (2005) for an account of how many of these factors played out in Bombay province in the formative years of Indian nationalism. The reference to "who should salute first, as to who should give way first" pertains to the Brahmin—Kayastha conflict (see Note 60 to 7.4).

109. The Bhagwat is the Bhagvad Gita. For a detailed discussion of the Bhagvad Gita by Ambedkar see "Krishna and His Gita" (BAWS 3). On how, for Ambedkar, the Bhagvad Gita is neither a book of religion nor a treatise on philosophy, see Pandit (1992). See also Kumar (2010) on "Ambedkar's attempt to retrieve a counterhistory of Indian antiquity".

110. "To be copied" in AoC 1936.

111. This is a war and diplomacy term. "One speaks of an armed neutrality when a neutral State take military measures for the purpose of defending its neutrality against possible or probable attempts of either belligerent [sic] to make use of the neutral territory" (Oppenheim 1905, 353).

112. Ambedkar, once again, is drawing on his mentor John Dewey whom he mentions and acknowledges later in the essay. Discussing the "need of a measure for the worth of any given mode of social life", Dewey writes (1916, ch. 7): "How numerous and varied are the interests which are consciously shared? How full and free is the interplay with other forms of association? If we apply these considerations to, say, a criminal band, we find that the ties which consciously hold the members together are few in number, reducible almost to a common interest in plunder; and that they are of such a nature as to isolate the group from other groups with respect to give and take of the values of life." See also Lenart Skof (2011) who maps the influence of Dewey's pragmatism on Ambedkar's political philosophy, tracks his debt to not just Dewey but also to British idealist and liberal TH. Green (1836-82), and connects this to the work of contemporary Brazilian philosopher and social theorist Roberto Mangabeira Unger, who taught Barack Obama at Harvard.

113. Thomas Carlyle (1795-1881) was a pre-eminent figure in Victorian letters. In History of the French Revolution (1837), he sympathised with the revolutionaries to an extent but despised anarchy, and appeared to fear the rule of the people. The concept of 'organic filaments' here is borrowed from Sartor Resartus (1833-4), a well-disguised autobiography and a critique of utilitarianism and British society, presenting fragments of Carlyle's philosophy in the form of a satire featuring a loose collection of papers written by a fictional German philosopher Diogenes Teufelsdr□ckh. In the seventh chapter of Book 3, Carlyle describes the world as a phoenix that begins to resurrect itself while dying. The 'organic filaments' are the processes of creation that hold together a world while it is destroying itself.

114. There has been a lot of recent research on caste among Muslims in India. Besides Imtiaz Ahmad (1978), see Ali Anwar's Masawat ki Jung [Battle for equality[7]] (2005) and Masood Alam Falahi's Hindustan mein zaat-paat aur Musalman [Casteism in India and Muslims] (2007). For a quick overview, see Khalid Anis Ansari (2013) who chronicles the contemporary pasmanda movement: "'Pasmanda', a Persian term meaning 'those who have fallen behind', refers to Muslims belonging to the Shudra (backward) and Ati-Shudra (Dalit) castes. It was adopted as an oppositional identity[7] to that of the dominant ashraf Muslims (forward castes) in 1998 by the Pasmanda Muslim Mahaz, a group which mainly worked in Bihar. Since then, however, the pasmanda discourse has found resonance elsewhere too."

115. On the practice of caste in Sikhism, see Notes 33 and 168 at 2.22 and 26.3.

116. This word does not figure in prior editions, and has been introduced for clarity.

117. S. Radhakrishnan (1888—1975) was a prolific writer, an apologist of Hinduism, and the second president of independent India. Ambedkar is citing from the book The Hindu Way of Life (1927, 12—13), a compilation of the lectures delivered at Oxford in 1926. Later in the work, Radhakrishnan says: "In dealing with the problem of the conflict of the different racial groups, Hinduism adopted the only[7] safe course of democracy, viz., that each racial group should be allowed to develop the best in it without

impeding the progress of others. Every historical group is unique and specific and has an ultimate value, and the highest morality requires that we should respect its individuality. Caste, on its racial side, is the affirmation of the infinite diversity of human groups" (97). Furthermore, "Caste was the answer of Hinduism to the forces pressing on it from outside. It was the instrument by which Hinduism civilised the different tribes it took in. Any group of people appearing exclusive in any sense is a caste. Whenever a group represents a type a caste arises" (104). Tellingly, his birth anniversary, 5 September, is celebrated as Teacher's Day in India.

118. AoC 1936: "impress the minds of many with the profundity of whatever he says."

119. These questions are given in bold in AoC 1936.

120. "Transit" in AoC 1936 and subsequent editions.

121. "Dravid" in all previous editions.

122. This is in bold in AoC 1936.

123. There has been a conventionally regarded division of labour between the laukika Brahmin, the so-called secular Brahmin, and the shrotriya or vaidika Brahmin, the Brahmin well versed in the Vedas (the shruti tradition; from sru, to hear, sro-triya; the oral tradition). The anthropologist M.N. Srinivas (1972, 8) uses these terms in this sense. The laukika—literally those who concern themselves with this-worldly, temporal (loka) matters—is not secular in the Western Enlightenment sense of the term, as in those who disavow belief or are free from religious rules and teachings. The laukika Brahmin— the Brahmin as minister, bureaucrat, civil servant, writer— whom Ambedkar goes on to refer as the intellectual class of the Hindus, pursues a non-priestly career; priestly work is the preserve of the vaidika/shrotriva Brahmins (again, priests who perform only Vedic rites are to be distinguished from priests who officiate in temples, attending to post-Bhakti, post-Vedic gods). Howeve r, the laukika Brahmin does not undermine the significance or role of the shrotriya Brahmin. In fact, he deploys and legitimises the services of the shrotriya Brahmin. The laukika Brahmin wields power over this-worldly matters, the shrotriya's domain is other-worldly. All the same, the laukika would even look down upon the shrotriya as lower in the pecking order; someone whose services can be easily bought, for a price. In effect, they are two flanks of

Brahminism. For a discussion on the etymology of laukika and vaidika in Sanskrit grammarian Panini's Ashtadhyayi (c. 400 BCE), see Patrick Olivelle (2008, 161-3).

124. Albert Venn Dicey (1835-1922) was a British jurist and constitutional theorist who expounded the theory of the 'rule of law' and popularised the term. The quote that follows is from Introduction to the Study of the Law of the Constitution (1885, 75—6) which forms a part of the unwritten British Constitution and is therefore also referred to as English Constitution.

125. Leslie Stephen (1832—1904) was a British philosopher, and literary and social critic. A referen to his comments on the prohibition of blue-eyed babies can be found in Dicey (1885, 78) cited above. Dicey is quoting Stephen from the Science of Ethics (1882), a work that sums up the ethical consequences of the theory of evolution.

126. Ambedkar is referring to the concept popularised by Carlyle in the nineteenth century: the great man theory. Carlyle's On Heroes, Hero-Worship and the Heroic in History (1840) points out the essential role of great men in history, such as Muhammad, Luther, Rousseau, Cromwell and Napoleon among others, as the moving force of history. The main criticism of the great man theory was formulated by Herbert Spencer in The Study of Sociology (1873), but Carlyle's theory has occupied the mind of many an influential thinker, for example Leo Tolstoy.

127. This is the injunction from the Manusmriti that Ambedkar cites at the opening of AoC. See Note at 1.2.

128. Shishthas: Brahmins educated in religious matters.

129. (Anaamnaateshu dharmeshu katham syaaditi chedbhavet/ yam shishtaa braahmanaa bruuyuh sa dharmah syaadashadgkitah.) Ambedkar first cites the translation of Manusmriti 12.108 from B□hler (1886/2004, 337) and then gives the Sanskrit verse. Bibek Debroy's translation: "If asked about parts of Dharma that have not been stated, without a doubt, what learned/good Brahmins state is Dharma."

130. It is not clear what Ambedkar is referring to as the ashtadhikaras. Adhikara, in both Vedic Hinduism and tantra, refers to the religious qualification and eligibility to perform certain rituals. According to James Lochtefeld (2002, 6), "This refers partly to

knowing how to perform the ritual, and thus being 'qualified' ... More importandy, it refers to having gained the ritual status that entitles one to perform the ritual. This status is usually conferred by some sort of formal initiation ... by one's teacher." Thus we may say Shambuka, the pivotal Shudra in the Ramayana, does not have the adhikara to perform a Vedic rite, and is hence punished. For further discussion of the idea of adhikara, see Wilhelm Halbfass (1990, 67), where he says "adhikara assumes such meanings as 'authority,' 'competence,' 'vocation,' but also 'obligation,' and 'responsibility' It refers to 'governing' functions and elements not only in nature or society, but also in texts and teachings, where it may indicate a governing rule or dominant theme."

131. Sanskaras (also samskaras) is the collective name given to various life-cycle sacrifices and rituals marking the different stages of human life; they are the rites that make people (or things) fit for a purpose (of performing rituals, taking one's rightful place in society), by removing taints and generating good qualities (Michaels, 2005, 74). Hindu Dharmashastras differ on the total number of sanskaras (twelve to eighteen) but sixteen sanskaras are generally agreed upon.
132. The word used in AoC 1936 is "silenced"; amended in 1937 and 1944 to "frozen instantly it is told". Edited here for clarity
133. In AoC 1936, this reads as "do not suffer equally"; amended in 1937.
134. This is the popularised version of one of the sentences from The Communist Manifesto (1848): "The proletarians have nothing to lose but their chains. They have a world to win. Working Men of All Countries, Unite!"
135. In AoC 1936: "you cannot use the slogan which Karl Marx used".
136. In AoC 1936, this sentence reads: "The Caste System is an imperium in imperio and in the general dissolution of Caste, some castes stand to lose more of their prestige and power than other castes." Imperium in imperio means a state, power or sovereignty within a state, power or sovereignty.
137. (Vedah smritih sadachara svasya cha priyamaatmana.) Debroy: "For his own self and for those who are loved by him, the Vedas, the Smritis and good conduct ..." This is a half of the shloka couplet. The complete shloka, from Manusmriti 2.12, is rendered

by B□hler as: "The Veda, the sacred tradition, the customs of virtuous men, and one's own pleasure, they declare to be visibly the fourfold means of defining the sacred law" (1886/2004, 19). The second line in Sanskrit reads as: (Etajna-chaturvidham praahu saakshadharmasya lakshanaam.)

138. Sadachar: Sanskrit for ethics or right behaviour, what Doniger and Smith render as "the conduct of good people". Ambedkar gives his explication in 22.14—15 of AoC.

139. (Yo-avamanyetateymuulehetushaastraashrayaatdvijah/ sa saadhubhirbahishkaaryo naastik vedanindakah.) Manusmriti 2.11. Debroy's translation: "Every dwija [it can be rendered as either Brahmin or belonging to the first three varnas] who depends on texts of logic and ignores these two sources [the earlier shloka mentions] must be banished by virtuous people, as a person who is a non-believer and as one who criticises the Vedas." Buhler's edition renders this as: "Every twice- born man, who, relying on the Institutes of dialectics, treats with contempt those two sources (of the law), must be cast out by the virtuous, as an atheist and a scorner of the Veda" (1886/2004,19).

140. At this point, in both AoC 1936 and 1937, Ambedkar introduces a verse from the Mahabharata, which in the 1944 edition he places later; see 22.7 in this edition: "The same rule is laid down in the Mahabharata:

141. In AoC 1936, the two sentences are conjoined with a "but", to read: "Either of them may be followed but no attempt ..." In 1937 and 1944, the "but" is removed.

142. (Shrutidvaidham tu yatra syaattatra dharmaavubhau smritau.) This is the first line of Manusmriti 2.14. Debroy's translation: "When there are two shruti texts that conflict, both are said to be Dharma." B□hler: "But when two sacred texts (shruti) are conflicting, both are held to be law; for both are pronounced by the wise (to be) valid law" (1886/2004, 20). Ambedkar paraphrases the verse after citing it.

143. (Yaa vedavaahyaah smrutayo yaashcha kaashcha kudrishtayah/ Smritisarvaastaa nishphalaa pretya tamonishthaa hi tah smritaah.) Manusmriti 12.95. Debroy: "All the smriti and other texts which are based on wicked doctrines and are outside the Vedas, lead to no fruits after death. It is said that they are based on darkness."

B□hler renders this as: "All those traditions (smriti) and those despicable systems of philosophy, which are not based on the Veda, produce no reward after death; for they are declared to be founded on Darkness" (1886/2004, 335).

144. Brihaspati was a Brahmin law-giver of the sixth or seventh century CE. Brihaspati's major wor t he Brihaspati Smriti, survives only in fragments. It has been published in The Minor Lawbooks (1889), translated by Julius Jolly. Brihaspati is considered the first Hindu law-giver to separate civil law from criminal law, and his views concerning women's rights are considered liberal. Nonetheless, he confers the death sentence on a man who has a sexual relationship with a 'high'- caste woman, while merely assigning fines for men who have a sexual relationship with a woman of equal or of 'lower' caste. Consent (or the absence of it) on the woman's part does not alter the severity of the punishment. See G.S. Ghurye (1969, 245).

145. (Vedaarthatvopanibandhutbaat praamaanyam hi manoh smritam/ Manvarthavipareeta tu ya smrutih saa na shasyatey.) Debroy: "In the first line of this verse there seems to be a typographic error. The first line should actually read (Vedaarthopanibaddhatvaat praadhaanyam tu manoh smrutam.) This is from the Vyavahara-kanda of Brihaspati Smriti. However, it is not from the main text; it is tagged on at the end of Vyavahara-kanda, chapter 1. The shloka therefore does not have a number." Debroy's translation: "But, for determining the boundaries of the meaning of the Vedas, Manu's smriti is pre-eminent. Any smriti that is contrary to Manu should not be taught/praised."

146. (Puraanam maanavo dharmah saango vedashchikitsitam/ Aajnaasiddhaani chatvaari na hantavyaani hetubhih.) Debroy: "This verse does not exist in the complete Critical Edition of the Mahabharata (Bhandarkar Oriental Research Institute, launched in 1966, ten years after Ambedkar's demise). Bhandarkar has it listed as 14.98—72 in the rejected texts, but there it occurs as the following, with a minor variation in the first word. That is, it is in Ashvamedhika parva, which does not figure in the Critical Edition: (Bhaaratammaanavodharmo vedaah saadgaashchikitsitam / Aajnaasiddhaani chatvaari na hantavyaani hetubhih.) A translation of the version Ambedkar uses: 'The Puranas, Manu's dharma, the Vedas and their limbs, and medicine— these four are in the nature

of commandments. Under no circumstances must they be killed/ destroyed.'"

147. Refer to the experiences of W.C. Bonnerjee discussed in Note 10 to AoC 2.6 as illustrative of Ambedkar's point.

148. Prayaschitta: Sanskrit for the purification rituals undertaken in penance after breaking caste taboos. It has also been variously understood as a combination of atonement, expiation and repentance. The Dharmashastras discuss prayaschitta (expiation) along with achara (ritual) and vyavahara (jurisprudence) as aspects of Hindu law.

149. The Slovenian Marxist philosopher Slavoj Zizek says of the Manusmriti and the caste system th such a system can be sustained "only by a complex panoply of tricks, displacements and compromises whose basic formula is that of universality with exceptions: in principle yes, but ... The Laws of Manu demonstrates a breath-taking ingenuity in accomplishing this task." □i□ek believes that the true regulating power of the law does not reside in its "direct prohibitions, in the division of our acts into permitted and prohibited, but in regulating the very violations of prohibitions: the law silently accepts that the basic prohibitions are violated (or even discreetly solicits us to violate them), and then, it tells us how to reconcile the violation with the law by way of violating the prohibition in a regulated way." Cited in S. Anand (2010). Ambedkar deals with this aspect later in his discussion of Annihilation of Caste with Gandhi featured in "A Reply to the Mahatma" (11.5), where he talks of how a Brahmin can remain a Brahmin irrespective of what he does: "The number of Brahmins who sell shoes is far greater than those who practise priesthood. Not only have the Brahmins given up their ancestral calling of priesthood for trading, but they have entered trades which are prohibited to them by the shastras. Yet how many Brahmins who break caste every day will preach against caste and against the shastras?" Wendy Doniger, in the introduction to her translation of the Manusmriti (Doniger and Smith, 1991, liv), talks of how it was "law in extremity", where every stringent rule has an exception that almost contradicts the rule; an emergency—apad—escape clause. "The concept of apad recognises human fallibility: don't do this, says Manu, but if you do, this is what to do to fix it."

150. Ramanuja, or Ramanujacharya, was a twelfth-century Brahmin philosopher, a proponent of the Vishishtadvaita, or qualified

monism, school of thought. Coming as he did after the monotheistic Tamil Bhakti movements of the Saivite Nayanmars and Vaishnavite Alwars (sixth to eighth centuries), Ramanuja gave primacy to Bhakti or worship of a personal god. In his commentary of the Brahma Sutra he declares the Shudra to be equally fit for studying the Vedas as the Brahmin and is said to have adopted a non-Brahmin as a guru. See Bartley (2002).

151. Kabir was a fifteenth-century radical saint-poet who was born a weaver; the thousands of songs/poems attributed to him question the caste system, declare equality in the eyes of god and promote Bhakti. See Hess and Singh (2002), and Hess (2009) for translations of Kabir. See www.kabirproject.org, curated by Shabnam Virmani, for an audio and video documentation of various Kabir traditions across the subcontinent.

152. (Yadhyaddaacharyateyena dharmyam vaa- adharmyameva vaa/ Deshasyaacharanam nityam charitram taddhikiirtitam.) Debroy says this verse has not been traceable since it does not say anything important enough for it to be cited or reproduced. Translation: "Whatever is followed in a country, be it dharma or be it adharma, that must always be observed and applauded."

153. Dharmya or adharmya. These terms broadly mean lawful/ sacred and unlawful. According to th Kautilya's Arthashastra, there are eight types of marriage, of which four are accorded dharmya status and the other four adharmya (1992, 394—5). For Ambedkar's discussion of these marriages, see "Riddle No. 19: The Change from Paternity to Maternity— What did the Brahmins Wish to Gain by it?" in Sharmila Rege (2013, 169-76).

154. (Yasmin deshe ya acharah paramparya-kramaagata / Varnanaam kila sarveshaam sa sadaachara uchyatey.) This almost echoes the previous verse Ambedkar cites. Debroy: "Whatever has been practised in whichever country, deriving from tradition, for all the varnas, is certainly said to be good conduct." This corresponds to Buhler's Manusmriti 2:18: "The custom handed down in regular succession (since time immemorial) among the (four chief) castes (varna) and the mixed (races) of that country, is called the conduct of virtuous men" (1886/2004, 20). However, the Sanskrit original does not use (Varnanam kila sarvesham) but (Varnanam saantaraalaanaam).

155. (Na deva charitamam charet.) Debroy: "One should not follow the conduct of the gods."

156. Once again, Ambedkar seems to be alluding to his mentor Dewey (1922, 239), who writes: "As habits set in grooves dominate activity and swerve it from conditions instead of increasing its adaptability, so principles treated as fixed rules instead of as helpful methods take men away from experience. The more complicated the situation, and the less we really know about it, the more insistent is the orthodox type of moral theory upon the prior existence of some fixed and universal principle or law which is to be directly applied and followed." There is a certain tension here between Dewey's words—who seems critical of rigid application of principles— and those of Ambedkar, who advocates sound principles as the only possible foundation for morality.

157. Jaimini's Purva Mimamsa Sutras, dated sometime between the second century BCE and secon century CE, is the first text in the Mimamsa school of philosophy, a school of exegesis concerned with the understanding of Vedic ritual injunctions. (Orthodox Hinduism has six schools of philosophy: Nyaya, Vaiseshika, Samkhya, Yoga, Mimamsa and Vedanta.) The Purva Mimamsa Sutras consists of a systematically ordered collection of approximately 2,745 short statements, also referred to individually as sutra. Ambedkar here is referring to sutra 1.1.2. For an account of the various explanations which have been offered for the terms 'Purva Mimamsa' and 'Uttara Mimamsa', see Parpola (1981). For a full translation of Purva Mimamsa Sutras with commentary, see Jha (1942); see also Benson (2010) and Clooney, S.J. (1990).

158. Edmund Burke (1729—97) was a British statesman, orator and political thinker of Irish origin. A staunch supporter of the American Revolution, he opposed the French Revolution in his work Reflections on the Revolution in France (1790). Ambedkar cites him often, especially during his interventions at the Round Table Conference (see Das 2010b). Though the source of this quotation has been difficult to trace, a fuller version of it has been widely cited. See O'Brien (1947, 191): "True religion is the foundation of society, the basis on which all true Civil Government rests and from which power derives its authority, laws their efficacy, and both their sanction. If it is once shaken by contempt, the whole fabric cannot be stable or lasting."

159. Sanad: Hindi for certificate or diploma. The Merriam- Webster dictionary gives the meaning of sanad as "an Indian government charter, warrant, diploma, patent or deed". Ambedkar's thoughts here on reform, and on giving a semblance of meritocracy to the institution of priesthood, gesture towards an alternate meaning of sanad as well. Isnaad (from Arabic sanad, 'support') in Islam is a list of authorities who have transmitted a report (hadith, also hadees) of a statement, action or approbation of Muhammad, one of his companions (sahaabah), or of a later authority (tabee); its reliability determines the validity of a hadith. The isnaad precedes the actual text (matn) and takes the form, "It has been related to me by A on the authority of B on the authority of C on the authority of D (usually a Companion of the Prophet) that Muhammad said ..." A careful scrutiny of the isnaads, rating each hadith according to the completeness of its chain of transmitters, and the reliability and orthodoxy of its authorities, was done in the second century AH (after 720 CE) to avoid confusion and multiple narrations, and to assist in giving precedence to the ahadith (the total body of hadith) over whatever local customs might have developed in Muslim communities (Scott 2004).

160. In AoC 1936 and 1937, this reads: "A priest should be the servant of the state like any civil servant and should be paid by the state." The italicised words are edited out in 1944.

161. It was the Bhagvad Gita—which Marxist historian D.D. Kosambi (1962, 16) says was added t the epic Mahabharata "somewhere between 150 and 350 AD"—that made the first popular case for the guna-karma theory. Here, guna means intrinsic qualities or attributes, and karma is actions. Much before the Gita, around the second century BCE, the Samkhya school of upanishadic philosophy propounded the tri-guna theory, the three gunas being sattva (corresponding to clarity of thought and purity of mind, associated with the Brahmin), rajas (passionate, excitable state of mind, associated with the Kshatriya) and tamas (darkness, a state of confusion, associated with the Shudra). Drawing on this Samkhya core, the Gita says in 4.13:

(Chaaturvanyaammayaahsrushtamgunakarmavibhaagasha: / Tasya kartaarama api maam viddhiya akartaaramavyayam.) Debroy (2005: 65) renders this as: "In accordance with gunas and action, the four varnas were created by me. But despite being the creator of these, know me to be constant and not the agent." This shloka makes the case that the varna attribute is determined by worth (guna) and action (karma) and not by birth as purported by the Rig Veda (hymns 11—12, Sukta 90, Book 10) and subsequently by Manu and other smritis. The Arya Samaj, and figures like Gandhi and Aurobindo, who sought to defend varnashrama but denounce jati, cited the guna—karma theory to say that caste need not be birth-based. Contrast this with how Ambedkar examines the origin and genesis of caste, and what he terms the System of Castes in his 1916 essay "Castes in India" (in Rege 2013). See also 16.4 and Note 92 on Plato's Republic.

162. This excerpt is from the first chapter, "What is Justice?", of Thomas Nixon Carver's Essays in Social Justice (1915, 20). Carver (1865-1961) was a neoclassical American economist who wrote on a wide array of topics such as rural economics, the problems of distribution of wealth, social justice, the place of religion in society, and social evolution. He was professor of economics and sociology at Harvard University from 1900 to 1932. Minor errors in Ambedkar's quotation of Carver— that perist in the 1936, 1937 and 1944 editions—have been corrected.
163. Towards the close of his address, Ambedkar records his debt to John Dewey from whose work as has been shown, he draws extensively. This being a presidential address at a conference it is understandable that Ambedkar does not alwavs cite references—not just from Dewey but for various other materials he marshals to make his case. This quote is from the second chapter of Democracy and Education: An Introduction to the Philosophy of Education (1916), concerning the role of the school in implementing social change.
164. Quote from Burke's Reflections on the Revolution in France (1790), in which he launched a bitter attack on the French Revolution.
165. Dewey, Democracy and Education, chapter 7.
166. Sanatan literally means eternal, everlasting; sanatan dharm (also rendered as sanatana dharma) i the religion that is said to have no beginning nor end. An orthodox person in the nationalist period would prefer to describe himself as someone who belonged to the 'sanatan dharm', the everlasting religion. The Anglicised terms 'Hindu' and 'Hinduism' do not capture the conservative fundamentalism inherent in sanatan dharm. While the Arya Samaj

or Brahmo Samaj advocated reforms, the sanatani Hindus (the orthodoxy) believed in an eternal/ sanatan Hinduism without any need for reforms. Ambedkar discusses Gandhi's sanatani tendencies in Appendix 9.30.

167. Much before right-wing Hindutva ideologue Arun Shourie (1997) suggested that Ambedkar was 'stooge' of the British and cast aspersions on his 'nationalist' credentials, the newspapers of Ambedkar's time constantly doubted his credentials. In What Congress and Gandhi Have Done to the Untouchables (BAWS 9, 200), Ambedkar writes: "[The Untouchables] have no Press and the Congress Press is closed to them. It is determined not to give them the slightest publicity. They cannot have their own Press. It is obvious that no paper can survive without advertisement revenue .... The staff of the Associated Press in India, which is the main news distributing agency in India, is entirely drawn from Madras Brahmins— indeed the whole of the Press in India is in their hands and who for well-known reasons are entirely pro-Congress and will not allow any news hostile to the Congress to get publicity. These are reasons beyond the control of the Untouchables." For a documentation of the insensitive way in which the so- called nationalist press reported on Ambedkar, see Ramnarayan Rawat (2001, 128-9).

168. The import here is that caste has contaminated even the new faiths that emerged from within Ind (such as Sikhism) as it did religions that came to India (Islam and Christianity). For an account of how caste affects Sikhism, see Mark Juergensmeyer (2009); on caste among Muslims in India, see Imtiaz Ahmad (1978); and among Christians, see Kenneth Ballhatchet (1998), and the more recent study focused on Tamil Nadu by David Mosse (2012).

169. Swaraj, literally 'self-rule', was the term used by the Congress party and other nationalist leade to refer to the struggle for independence from British rule. The conservative leader Bal Gangadhar Tilak famously declared in 1899: "Swaraj is my birthright, and I shall have it!" However, it was Gandhi who popularised the term, especially with his manifestolike Hind Swaraj or Indian Home Rule (1909). According to Gandhi, "It is swaraj when we learn to rule ourselves." For an annotated edition of Hind Swaraj, see Parel (1997). According to Lelyveld (2011,

xiv), swaraj for Gandhi was bigger than the struggle for mere independence from British rule. "As used by Gandhi, poorna [complete] swaraj put the goal on yet a higher plane. At his most utopian, it was a goal not just for India but for each individual Indian; only then could it be poorna, or complete. It meant a sloughing not only of British rule but of British ways, a rejection of modern industrial society in favor of a bottom-up renewal of India, starting in its villages ..."

170. Echoing a similar sentiment in 1927, when he led the civil rights struggle for Untouchables' access to the Chavadar Tank in Mahad, Ambedkar said: "The satyagraha movement started by Gandhi was backed by the people as it was against foreign domination. Our struggle is against the mass of caste Hindus and naturally we have little support from outside." Excerpts of Ambedkar's speech in Mahad, where he compares the event to the storming of the Bastille, can be found in Arjun Dangle (1992, 223—33) and in Satyanarayana and Tharu (2013, 22—31). For an account of the Mahad struggle, see Zelliot (2013, 78-82) and Rao (2009, 83-8).

The Ambedkar—Gandhi Debate

A Vindication of Caste by Mahatma Gandhi Dr Ambedkar's Indictment—1

1

1.11

The readers will recall the fact that Dr Ambedkar was to have presided last May at the annual conference of the Jat- Pat Todak Mandal of Lahore. But the conference itself was cancelled because Dr Ambedkar's address was found by the reception committee to be unacceptable. How far a reception committee is justified in rejecting a president of its choice because of his address that may be objectionable to it is open to question. The committee knew Dr Ambedkar's views on caste and the Hindu scriptures. They knew also that he had in unequivocal terms decided to give up Hinduism. Nothing less than the address that Dr Ambedkar had prepared was to be expected from him. The committee appears to have deprived the public of an opportunity of listening to the original views of a man who has carved out for himself a unique position in society. Whatever label he wears in future, Dr Ambedkar is not the man to allow himself to be forgotten.

1.2

Dr Ambedkar was not going to be beaten by the reception committee. He has answered their rejection of him by publishing the address at his own expense. He has priced it at 8 annas, I would suggest a reduction to 2 annas or at least 4 annas.

1.3

No reformer can ignore the address. The orthodox will gain by reading it. This is not to say that the address is not open to objection. It has to be read only because it is open to serious objection. Dr Ambedkar is a challenge to Hinduism. Brought up as a Hindu, [3] educated by a Hindu potentate,[4] he has become so disgusted with the so-called savarna Hindus or the treatment that he and his people have received at their hands that he proposes to leave not only them but the very religion that is his and their common heritage. He has transferred to that religion his disgust against a part of its professors.

1.4

But this is not to be wondered at. After all, one can only judge a system or an institution by the conduct of its representatives. What is more, Dr Ambedkar found that the vast majority of savarna Hindus had not only conducted themselves inhumanly against those of their fellow religionists whom they classed as Untouchables, but they had based their conduct on the authority of their scriptures, and when he began to search them he had found ample warrant for their beliefs in untouchability and all its implications. The author of the address has quoted chapter and verse in proof of his three-fold indictment—inhuman conduct itself, the unabashed justification for it on the part of the perpetrators, and the subsequent discovery that the justification was warranted by their scriptures.

1.5

No Hindu who prizes his faith above life itself can afford to underrate the importance of this indictment. Dr Ambedkar is not alone in his disgust. He is its most uncompromising exponent and one of the ablest among them. He is certainly the most irreconcilable among them. Thank god, in the front rank of the leaders he is singularly alone, and as yet but a representative of a very small minority. But what he says is voiced with more or less vehemence by many leaders belonging to the Depressed Classes. Only the latter, for instance Rao Bahadur M.C. Rajah and Dewan Bahadur Srinivasan,[5] not only do not threaten to give up Hinduism, but find enough warmth in it to compensate for the shameful persecution to which the vast mass of Harijans are exposed.

1.6

But the fact of many leaders remaining in the Hindu fold is no warrant for disregarding what Dr Ambedkar has to say. The savarnas have to correct their belief and their conduct. Above all, those who are, by their learning and influence, among the savarnas have to give an authoritative interpretation of the scriptures. The questions that Dr Ambedkar's indictment suggests are:

1. What are the scriptures?
2. Are all the printed texts to be regarded as an integral part of them, or is any part of them to be rejected as unauthorised interpolation?
3. What is the answer of such accepted and expurgated scriptures on the question of untouchability, caste, equality of status, inter-dining and intermarriages? (These have been all examined by Dr Ambedkar in his address.)

I must reserve for the next issue my own answer to these questions and a statement of the (at least some) manifest flaws in Dr Ambedkar's thesis.

Harijan, 11 July 1936

Dr Ambedkar's Indictment—2

2

2.1

The Vedas, Upanishads, smritis and puranas, including the Ramayana and the Mahabharata, are the Hindu scriptures. Nor is this a finite list. Every age or even generation has added to the list. It follows, therefore, that everything printed or even found handwritten is not scripture. The smritis, for instance, contain much that can never be accepted as the word of God. Thus many of the texts that Dr Ambedkar quotes from the smritis cannot be accepted as authentic. The scriptures, properly so called, can only be concerned with eternal verities and must appeal to any conscience, i.e., any heart whose eyes of understanding are opened. Nothing can be accepted as the word of God which cannot be tested by reason or be capable of being spiritually experienced. And even when you have an expurgated edition of the scriptures, you will need their interpretation. Who is the best interpreter? Not learned men surely. Learning there must be. But religion does not live by it. It lives in the experiences of its saints and seers, in their lives and sayings. When all the most learned commentators of the scriptures are utterly forgotten, the accumulated experience of the sages and saints will abide and be an inspiration for ages to come.

2.2

Caste has nothing to do with religion. It is a custom whose origin I do not know, and do not need to know for the satisfaction of my spiritual hunger. But I do know that it is harmful both to spiritual and national growth. Varna and ashrama[6] are institutions which have nothing to do with castes. The law of varna teaches us that we have each one of us to earn our bread by following the ancestral calling. It defines not our rights but our duties. It necessarily has reference to callings that are conducive to the welfare of humanity and to no other. It also follows that there is no calling too low and none too high. All are good, lawful and absolutely equal in status. The callings of a Brahmin—spiritual teacher—and a scavenger are equal, and their due performance carries equal merit before God, and at one time seems to have carried identical reward before man. Both were entitled to their livelihood and no more. Indeed one traces even now in the villages the faint lines of this healthy operation of the law.[7]

2.3

Living in Segaon [8] with its population of six hundred, I do not find a great disparity between the earnings of different tradesmen, including Brahmins. I find too that real Brahmins are to be found, even in these degenerate days, who are living on alms freely given to them and are giving freely of what they have of spiritual treasures. It would be wrong and improper to judge the law of varna by its caricature in the lives of men who profess to belong to a varna, whilst they openly commit a breach of its only operative rule. Arrogation of a superior status by and of a varna over another is a denial of the law. And there is nothing in the law of varna to warrant a belief in untouchability. (The essence of Hinduism is contained in its enunciation of one and only God as truth and its bold acceptance of ahimsa as the law of the human family.)

2.4

I am aware that my interpretation of Hinduism will be disputed by many besides Dr Ambedkar. That does not affect my position. It is an interpretation by which I have lived for nearly half a century, and according to which I have endeavoured to the best of my ability to regulate my life.

2.5

In my opinion the profound mistake that Dr Ambedkar has made in his address is to pick out the texts of doubtful authenticity and value, and the state of degraded Hindus who are no fit specimens of the faith they so woefully misrepresent. Judged by the standard applied by Dr Ambedkar every known living faith will probably fail.

2.6

In his able address, the learned doctor has over-proved his case. Can a religion that was professed by Chaitanya, Jnyandeo, Tukaram, Tiruvalluvar, Ramakrishna Paramahansa, Raja Ram Mohan Roy, Maharshi Devendranath Tagore, Vivekananda,[9] and a host of others who might be easily mentioned, be so utterly devoid of merit as is made out in Dr Ambedkar's address? A religion has to be judged not by its worst specimens but by the best it might have produced. For that and that alone can be used as the standard to aspire to, if not to improve upon.

Harijan, 18 July 1936

Sant Ram responds to Gandhi Varna versus Caste

3

3.1

Shri Sant Ramji of the Jat-Pat Todak Mandal of Lahore wants me to publish the following:[10]

3.2

"I have read your remarks about Dr Ambedkar and the Jat- Pat Todak Mandal, Lahore. In that connection I beg to submit as follows:

"We did not invite Dr Ambedkar to preside over our conference because he belonged to the Depressed Classes, for we do not distinguish between a Touchable and an Untouchable Hindu. On the contrary our choice fell on him simply because his diagnosis of the fatal disease of the Hindu community was the same as ours, i.e., he too was of the opinion that the caste system was the root cause of the disruption and downfall of the Hindus. The subject of the doctor's thesis for his doctorate being the caste system,[11] he has studied the subject thoroughly. Now the object of our conference was to persuade the Hindus to annihilate caste, but the advice of a non-Hindu in social and religious matters can have no effect on them. The doctor in the supplementary portion of his address insisted on saying that that was his last speech as a Hindu,[12] which was irrelevant as well as pernicious to the interests of the conference. So we requested him to expunge that sentence, for he could easily say the same thing on any other occasion. But he refused, and we saw no utility in making merely a show of our function. In spite of all this, I cannot help praising his address, which is, as far as I know, the most learned thesis on the subject and worth translating into every vernacular of India.

3.3

"Moreover, I want to bring to your notice that your philosophical difference between caste and varna is too subtle to be grasped by people in general, because for all practical purposes in Hindu society, caste and varna are one and the same thing, for the function of both of them is one and the same, i.e. to restrict inter-caste marriages and inter-dining. Your theory of varnavyavastha is impracticable in this age, and there is no hope of its revival in the near future. But Hindus are slaves of caste, and do not want to destroy it. So when you advocate your ideal of imaginary varnavyavastha, they find justification for clinging to caste. Thus you are doing a great disservice to social reform by advocating your imaginary utility of the division of varnas, for it creates a hindrance in our way. To try to remove untouchability without striking at the root of varnavyavastha is simply to treat the outward symptoms of a disease, or to draw a line on the surface of water. As in the heart of their hearts dwijas do not want to give social equality to the so-called Touchable and Untouchable Shudras, so they refuse to break caste—and give liberal donations for the removal of untouchability simply to evade the issue. To seek the help of the shastras for the removal of untouchability and caste is simply to wash mud with mud."

3.4

The last paragraph of the letter surely cancels the first. If the Mandal rejects the help of the shastras, they do exactly what Dr Ambedkar does, i.e., cease to be Hindus. How then can they object to Dr Ambedkar's address merely because he said that that was his last speech as a Hindu? The position appears to be wholly untenable, especially when the Mandal, for which Shri Sant Ram claims to speak, applauds the whole argument of Dr Ambedkar's address.

3.5

But it is pertinent to ask what the Mandal believes in, if it rejects the shastras. How can a Muslim remain one if he rejects the Quran, or a Christian remain Christian if he rejects the Bible? If caste and varna are convertible terms, and if varna is an integral part of the shastras which define Hinduism, I do not know how a person who rejects caste, i.e., varna, can call himself a Hindu.

3.6

Shri Sant Ram likens the shastras to mud. Dr Ambedkar has not, so far as I remember, given any such picturesque name to the shastras. I have certainly meant when I have said: that if shastras support the existing untouchability I should cease to call myself a Hindu. Similarly, if the shastras support caste, as we know it today in all its hideousness, I may not call myself or remain a Hindu, since I have no scruples about inter-dining or intermarriage. I need not repeat my position regarding shastras and their interpretation. I venture to suggest to Shri Sant Ram that it is the only rational and correct and morally defensible position, and it has ample warrant in Hindu tradition.

Harijan, 15 August 1936

Notes

1. The title given by Gandhi to his two-part response to AoC, published first in Harijan, was "Dr Ambedkar's Indictment". Ambedkar includes Gandhi's response in the revised 1937 edition of AoC and gives it his own title "A Vindication of Caste by Mahatma Gandhi". While Sant Ram's rejoinder to Gandhi was published in Harijan, Ambedkar chose to publish his own exhaustive reply to Gandhi in the 1937 edition. All these are sequentiallv arranged here as they appear in AoC 1937.
2. Primary membership to the Congress party cost four annas.
3. Gandhi 'moved from truth to truth' on Ambedkar's identity and the motives for his commitment t anticaste struggle. Shortly before the Round Table Conference, when they first met in Bombay, Gandhi took Ambedkar to be a radical Brahmin fighting untouchability. As his grandson Rajmohan Gandhi notes in his biography of Gandhi (2007, 334), Gandhi did not, however, say this to Ambedkar, and quickly realised his mistake.
4. The reference is to the Maharaja of Baroda, Sayajirao Gaekwad (1863—1939), who pioneered social reform by opening eighteen special schools for Untouchables in his state, and supported Ambedkar's education—both in India (with a stipend of twenty-five rupees for Ambedkar's B.A. at Elphinstone College, Bombay) and abroad (his M.. and Ph.D. at Columbia University, on a scholarship of 11.5 British pounds per month for three years, in 1913—16). See Fatehsinhrao Gaekwad's (1989) biography of Maharaja Sayajirao III.
5. Rao Bahadur M.C. Rajah (1883-1943) and Rettamalai Srinivasan (1860—1945, conferred the ti Dewan Bahadur) were Untouchable

leaders from Madras Presidency. Rajah— author of The Oppressed Hindus (1925), the first ever book in English by an Untouchable in India—was the chief poEtical rival of Ambedkar to the position of the representative of the Depressed Classes on the national scene. Like Ambedkar, his grandfather served the British army. In 1922, Rajah was conferred the British honorary title, Rao Bahadur, after his entrance to the Madras Legislative Council as the first Adi Dravida (as Untouchables were known in Tamil-speaking areas) member. In 1927, he became the first Depressed Classes member to be nominated to the Central Legislative Council. Rajah was piqued that Ambedkar chose Srinivasan, also a member of the Madras Legislative Council, over him as a delegate to the Round Table Conference. Srinivasan accompanied Ambedkar to the two Round Table Conferences, in 1930 and 1931. He testified alongside Ambedkar to the Simon Commission, and followed him in the demand for separate electorates. In 1932, during the negotiations after the 1931 Round Table Conference, Rajah aligned himself with B.S. Moonje of the Hindu Mahasabha and came up with the Rajah—Moonje Pact guaranteeing reserved seats for Depressed Classes in a joint electorate with Hindus; this was vehemently rejected by the All-India Depressed Classes Conference held at Nagpur. Depressed Class groups across India threw in their lot with Ambedkar. Rajah came to regret his position much later. When Ambedkar was browbeaten into signing the Poona Pact in September 1932, the arrangement was in fact not so different from the Rajah-Moonje Pact. As Jaffrelot (2005, 67) notes: "This scheme was in fact close to that advocated by the Rajah—Moonje pact. For Gandhi, the Poona Pact was much more than an exercise in political engineering: it had wider implications for society as a whole, as evident from his comment to Ambedkar in 1933: 'In accepting the Poona Pact you accept the position that you are Hindus.'" Three years later, goaded by Gandhians and the Mahasabha, Rajah even denounced Ambedkar's announcement that he would not die a Hindu. For an account of how Rajah was manipulated by Gandhi in this, see Keer (1954/1990, 266-84). See also Zelliot (2013, 124—39). However, as jaffrelot notes: "Rajah was to join Ambedkar six years later, in 1938, after having been dismayed by the conservatism of the government formed by Congress in his province of Madras. He complained about it to Gandhi, who advised him to be patient and reaffirmed his confidence in the leader of the Madras government, a Brahmin, Rajagopalachari. Rajah, demoralised, thus came to regret the Poona Pact, and opposed, like Ambedkar, the Quit India Movement of 1942" (2005, 181-2 n48). Further, the proposals made by the Cripps Mission in 1942 caused "M.C. Rajah to become still closer to Ambedkar. Like him, he regretted the absence, in this set of proposals, of a provision granting a separate electorate to Untouchables ... During his tour in the south, in 1944, Ambedkar was invited by M.C. Rajah to Madras" (184 n31).

6. Just like human beings are divided into four varnas, a 'twice-born' savarna Hindu male's life h four stages (ashramas), ascending from the status of brahmacharva (unmarried, where man devotes his time to education), grihastha (householder), and vanaprastha (he dwells in the forest as a hermit but without severing ties with his family) to sannvasa (total renunciation of the world). The Manusmriti, among other Hindu scriptures, discusses the ashramas at length.
7. Gandhi here is restating his views on the benefits of varnashrama explicated by him in one of hi earlier writings (Young India, 13 August 1925; CWMG 32, 286), in which he says: "Varnashrama, in my opinion, was not conceived in any narrow spirit. On the contrary, it gave the labourer, the Shudra, the same status as the thinker, the Brahmin." Even earlier, he wrote (Young India , 25 February 1920; CWMG 19, 417): "I am one of those who do not consider caste to be a harmful institution. In its origin, caste was a wholesome custom and promoted national well-being. In my opinion, the idea that inter-dining or intermarrying is necessary for national growth, is a superstition borrowed from the West." While later coming around to criticising caste/jati as a corruption, throughout his life Gandhi steadfasdy defended an 'idealised' varnavyavastha (varna system). Nauriya (2006) believes that Gandhi came to recant his views on varnashrama.
8. Segaon: later called Sevagram, the ashram established by Gandhi, near Wardha (in today's Maharashtra).
9. Chaitanya was a Vaishnava saint from sixteenth-century Bengal, a proponent of Bhakti yoga. Jnyandeo, or Gyandev (also Dnyandev), was a thirteenth-century Bhakti poet-saint from western India; he wrote a commentary on the Bhagvad Gita. Tukaram was a seventeenth- century sant of the Varkari tradition; Cokhamela

was a fourteenth0century Mahar sant of the same tradition (not mentioned by Gandhi). Tiruvalluvar was a Tamil poet and philosopher, the author of the Thirukkural, from sometime between the second and eighth centuries CE. Ramakrishna Paramahansa was a nineteenth-century Kali worshipping mystic from Bengal. Raja Ram Mohan Roy and Maharshi Devendranath Tagore together founded the Brahmo Samaj, a social and religious reform movement in nineteenthcentury Bengal (Kopf 1979). Vivekananda was a self-styled Hindu monk. A disciple of Ramakrishna Paramahansa, he founded the Ramakrishna Mission (see Sharma 2012).

10. Gandhi published Sant Ram's letter in Harijan and appended his own response to it.
11. While Ambedkar did write a paper called "Castes in India" in 1916 during his years in Columb University, the subject of his doctoral dissertation was not the caste system. His doctoral work was on The Evolution of Provincial Finance in British India: A Study in the Provincial Decentralisation of Imperial Finance, and it was later published by P.S. King and Co., London, in 1925, with a foreword by Edwin Seligman who taught Ambedkar at Columbia.
12. This seems to be a deliberate misreading of what Ambedkar actually says in his speech, made n only by Sant Ram but also Har Bhagwan (see his letter to Ambedkar in the Prologue to AoC). While Ambedkar did denounce Hinduism and declared he would walk out of the Hindu fold in 1935 (see Note 15 to Prologue of AoC), the exact words of Ambedkar in AoC 25.1 are "this would probably be my last address to a Hindu audience, on a subject vitally concerning the Hindus" (emphasis added).

A Reply to the Mahatma

B.R. Ambedkar

1

1.1

1 appreciate greatly the honour done me by the Mahatma in taking notice in his Harijan of the speech on caste which I had prepared for the Jat-Pat Todak Mandal. From a perusal of his review of my speech, it is clear that the Mahatma completely dissents from the views I have expressed on the subject of caste. I am not in the habit of entering into controversy with my opponents unless there are special reasons which compel me to act otherwise. Had my opponent been some mean and obscure person I would not have pursued him. But my opponent being the Mahatma himself, I feel I must attempt to meet the case to the contrary which he has sought to put forth.

1.2

While I appreciate the honour he has done me, I must confess to a sense of surprise on finding that of all people the Mahatma should accuse me of a desire to seek publicity, as he seems to do when he suggests that in publishing the undelivered speech my object was to see that I was not 'forgotten'. Whatever the Mahatma may choose to say, mv object in publishing the speech was to provoke the Hindus to think, and to take stock of their position. I have never hankered for publicity, and if I may say so, I have more of it than I wish or need. But supposing it was out of the motive of gaining publicity that I printed the speech, who could cast a stone at me? Surely not those who, like the Mahatma, live in glass houses.

2

2.1

Motive apart, what has the Mahatma to say on the question raised by me in the speech? First of all, anyone who reads my speech will realise that the Mahatma has entirely missed the issues raised by me, and that the issues he has raised are not the issues that arise out of what he is pleased to call mv indictment of the Hindus. The principal points which I have tried to make out in my speech may be catalogued as follows:

2.2

(1) That caste has ruined the Hindus; (2) that the reorganisation of Hindu society on the basis of chaturvarnya is impossible because the varnavyavastha is like a leaky pot or like a man running at the nose. [1] It is incapable of sustaining itself by its own virtue and has

an inherent tendency to degenerate into a caste system unless there is a legal sanction behind it which can be enforced against everyone transgressing his varna; (3) that the reorganisation of Hindu society on the basis of chaturvarnya would be harmful, because the effect of the varnavyavastha would be to degrade the masses by denying them opportunity to acquire knowledge and to emasculate them by denying them the right to be armed; (4) that Hindu society must be reorganised on a religious basis which would recognise the principles of liberty, equality and fraternity; (5) that in order to achieve this object the sense of religious sanctity behind caste and varna must be destroyed; (6) that the sanctity of caste and varna can be destroyed only by discarding the divine authority of the shastras.

2.3

It will be noticed that the questions raised by the Mahatma are absolutely besides the point, and show that the main argument of the speech was lost upon him.

3

3.1

Let me examine the substance of the points made by the Mahatma. The first point made by the Mahatma is that the texts cited by me are not authentic. I confess I am no authority on this matter. But I should like to state that the texts cited by me are all taken from the writings of the late Mr Tilak, [2] who was a recognised authority on the Sanskrit language and on the Hindu shastras. His second point is that these shastras should be interpreted not by the learned but by the saints; and that as the saints have understood them the shastras do not support caste and untouchability.

3.2

As regards the first point, what I would like to ask the Mahatma is, what does it avail to anyone if the texts are interpolations, and if they have been differently interpreted by the saints? The masses do not make any distinction between texts which are genuine and texts which are interpolations. The masses do not know what the texts are. They are too illiterate to know the contents of the shastras. They have believed what they have been told, and what they have been told is that the shastras do enjoin as a religious duty the observance of caste and untouchability.

3.3

With regard to the saints, one must admit that howsoever different and elevating their teachings may have been as compared to those of the merely learned, they have been lamentably ineffective. They have been ineffective for two reasons. Firstly, none of the saints ever attacked the caste system. On the contrary—they were staunch believers in the system of castes. Most of them lived and died as members of the castes to which they respectively belonged. So passionately attached was Jnyandeo to his status as a Brahmin that when the Brahmins of Paithan would not admit him to their fold, he moved heaven and earth to get his status as a Brahmin recognised by the Brahmin fraternity.

3.4

And even the saint Eknath,[3] who now figures in the film Dharmatma[4] as a hero for having shown the courage to touch the Untouchables and dine with them, did so not because he was opposed to caste and untouchability, but because he felt that the pollution caused thereby could be washed away by a bath in the sacred waters of the river Ganges. [5] The saints have never, according to my study, carried on a campaign against caste and untouchability. They were not concerned with the struggle between men. They were concerned with the relation between man and god. They did not preach that all men were equal. They preached that all men were equal in the eyes of god—a very different and a very innocuous proposition, which nobody can find difficult to preach or dangerous to believe in.[6]

3.5

The second reason why the teachings of the saints proved ineffective was because the masses have been taught that a saint might break caste, but the common man must not. A saint therefore never became an example to follow. He always remained a pious man to be honoured. That the masses have remained staunch believers in caste and untouchability shows that the pious lives and noble sermons of the saints have had no effect on their life and conduct, as against the teachings of the shastras. Thus it can be a matter of no consolation that there were saints, or that there is a Mahatma who understands the shastras differendy from the learned few or ignorant many.[7]

3.6

That the masses hold a different view of the shastras is a fact which should and must be reckoned with. How that is to be dealt with, except by denouncing the authority of the shastras which continue to govern their conduct, is a question which the Mahatma has not considered. But whatever the plan the

Mahatma puts forth as an effective means to free the masses from the teachings of the shastras, he must accept that the pious life led by one good Samaritan may be very elevating to himself, but in India, with the attitude the common man has to saints and to Mahatmas —to honour but not to follow— one cannot make much out of it.

4

4.1

The third point made by the Mahatma is that a religion professed by Chaitanya, Jnyandeo, Tukaram, Tiruvalluvar, Ramakrishna Paramahansa, etc., cannot be devoid of merit as is made out by me, and that a religion has to be judged not by its worst specimens but by the best it might have produced. I agree with every word of this statement. But I do not quite understand what the Mahatma wishes to prove thereby. That religion should be judged not by its worst specimens but by its best is true enough, but does it dispose of the matter? I say it does not.

4.2

The question still remains, why the worst number so many and the best so few. To my mind there are two conceivable answers to this question: (1) that the worst by reason of some original perversity of theirs are morally uneducable, and are therefore incapable of making the remotest approach to the religious ideal. Or: (2) that the religious ideal is a wholly wrong ideal which has given a wrong moral twist to the lives of the many, and that the best have become best in spite of the wrong ideal—in fact, by giving to the wrong twist a turn in the right direction.

4.3

Of these two explanations I am not prepared to accept the first, and I am sure that even the Mahatma will not insist upon the contrary. To my mind the second is the only logical and reasonable explanation, unless the Mahatma has a third alternative to explain why the worst are so many and the best so few. If the second is the only explanation, then obviously the argument of the Mahatma that a religion should be judged by its best followers carries us nowhere—except to pity the lot of the many who have gone wrong because they have been made to worship wrong ideals.

5

5.1

The argument of the Mahatma that Hinduism would be tolerable if only many were to follow the example of the saints is fallacious for another reason. (In this connection, see the illuminating article on "Morality and the Social Structure" by H.N. Brailsford in the Aryan Path for April 1936. [8]) By citing the names of such illustrious persons as Chaitanya, etc., what the Mahatma seems to me to suggest in its broadest and simplest form is that Hindu society can be made tolerable and even happy without any fundamental change in its structure, if all the high-caste Hindus can be persuaded to follow a high standard of morality in their dealings with the low- caste Hindus. I am totally opposed to this kind of ideology.

5.2

I can respect those of the caste Hindus who try to realise a high social ideal in their life. Without such men, India would be an uglier and a less happy place to live in than it is. But nonetheless, anyone who relies on an attempt to turn the members of the caste Hindus into better men by improving their personal character is, in my judgement, wasting his energy and hugging an illusion. Can personal character make the maker of armaments a good man, i.e., a man who will sell shells that will not burst and gas that will not poison? If it cannot, how can you accept personal character to make a man loaded with the consciousness of caste a good man, i.e., a man who would treat his fellow men as his friends and equals? To be true to himself he must deal with his fellow man either as a superior or inferior, according as the case may be; at any rate, differently from his own caste-fellows. He can never be expected to deal with his fellow men as his kinsmen and equals.

5.3

As a matter of fact, a Hindu does treat all those who are not of his caste as though they were aliens, who could be discriminated against with impunity, and against whom any fraud or trick may be practised without shame. This is to say that there can be a better or a worse Hindu. But a good Hindu there cannot be. This is so not because there is anything wrong with his personal character. In fact, what is wrong is the entire basis of his relationship to his fellows. The best of men cannot be moral if the basis of relationship between them and their fellows is fundamentally a wrong relationship. To a slave, his master may be better or worse. But there cannot be a good master. A good man cannot be a master, and a master cannot be a good man.

5.4

The same applies to the relationship between high caste and low caste. To a low-caste man, a high-caste man can be better or worse as compared to other high-caste men. A high- caste man cannot be a good man, in so far as he must have a low caste man to distinguish him as a high-caste man. It cannot be good to a low-caste man to be conscious that there is a high-caste man above him. I have argued in my speech that a society based on varna or caste is a society which is based on a wrong relationship. I had hoped that the Mahatma would attempt to demoEsh my argument. But instead of doing that, he has merely reiterated his belief in chaturvarnya without disclosing the ground on which it is based.

6

6.1

Does the Mahatma practise what he preaches? One does not like to make personal reference in an argument which is general in its application. But when one preaches a doctrine and holds it as a dogma there is a curiosity to know how far he practises what he preaches. It may be that his failure to practise is due to the ideal being too high to be attainable; it may be that his failure to practise is due to the innate hypocrisy of the man. In any case he exposes his conduct to examination, and I must not be blamed if I ask how far has the Mahatma attempted to realise his ideal in his own case?

6.2

The Mahatma is a Bania trader by birth. His ancestors had abandoned trading in favour of ministership, which is a calling of the Brahmins. In his own life, before he became a Mahatma, when the occasion came for him to choose his career he preferred law to scales. On abandoning law, he became half saint and half politician. He has never touched trading, which is his ancestral calling.

6.3

His youngest son—I take the one who is a faithful follower of his father—was born a Vaishya, has married a Brahmin's daughter, and has chosen to serve a newspaper magnate. [9] The Mahatma is not known to have condemned him for not following his ancestral calling. It may be wrong and uncharitable to judge an ideal by its worst specimens. But surely the Mahatma as a specimen is no better, and if he even fails to realise the ideal then the ideal must be an impossible ideal, quite opposed to the practical instincts of man.

6.4

Students of Carlyle know that he often spoke on a subject before he thought about it. I wonder whether such has not been the case with the Mahatma in regard to the subject matter of caste. Otherwise, certain questions which occur to me would not have escaped him. When can a calling be deemed to have become an ancestral calling, so as to make it binding on a man? Must a man follow his ancestral calling even if it does not suit his capacities, even when it has ceased to be profitable? Must a man live by his ancestral calling even if he finds it to be immoral? If everyone must pursue his ancestral calling, then it must follow that a man must continue to be a pimp because his grandfather was a pimp, and a woman must continue to be a prostitute because her grandmother was a prostitute. Is the Mahatma prepared to accept the logical conclusion of his doctrine? To me his ideal of following one's ancestral calling is not only an impossible andimpractical ideal, but it is also morally an indefensible ideal.

7

7.1

The Mahatma sees great virtue in a Brahmin remaining a Brahmin all his life. Leaving aside the fact that there are many Brahmins who do not like to remain Brahmins all their lives, what can we say about those Brahmins who have clung to their ancestral calling of priesthood? Do they do so from any faith in the virtue of the principle of ancestral calling, or do they do so from motives of filthy lucre? The Mahatma does not seem to concern himself with such queries. He is satisfied that these are "real Brahmins who are living on alms freely given to them, and giving freely what they have of spiritual treasures". This is how a hereditary Brahmin priest appears to the Mahatma—a carrier of spiritual treasures.

7.2

But another portrait of the hereditary Brahmin can also be drawn. A Brahmin can be a priest to Vishnu—the god of love. He can be a priest to Shankar—the god of destruction. He can be a priest at Buddha Gaya[10] worshipping Buddha—the greatest teacher of mankind, who taught the noblest doctrine of love. He also can be a priest to Kali, the goddess who must have a daily sacrifice of an animal to satisfy her thirst for blood. He will be a priest of the temple of Rama—the Kshatriya god! He will also be a priest of the temple of Parshuram, the god who took on an avatar to destroy the Kshatriyas! He can be a priest to Brahma, the creator of the world. He can be a priest to a pir,[11] whose god Allah will not brook the claim of Brahma to share his spiritual dominion over the world! No one can say that this is a picture which is not true to life.

7.3

If this is a true picture, one does not know what to say of this capacity to bear loyalties to gods and goddesses whose attributes are so antagonistic that no honest man can be a devotee to all of them. The Hindus rely upon this extraordinary phenomenon as evidence of the greatest virtue of their religion—namely, its catholicity, its spirit of toleration. As against this facile view, it can be urged that what is toleration and catholicity may be really nothing more creditable than indifference or flaccid latitudinarianism. These two attitudes are hard to distinguish in their outer seeming. But they are so vitally unlike in their real quality that no one who examines them closely can mistake one for the other.

7.4

That a man is ready to render homage to many gods and goddesses may be cited as evidence of his tolerant spirit. But can it not also be evidence of an insincerity born of a desire to serve the times? I am sure that this toleration is merely insincerity. If this view is well founded, one may ask, what spiritual treasure can there be within a person who is ready to be a priest and a devotee to any deity which it serves his purpose to worship and to adore? Not only must such a person be deemed to be bankrupt of all spiritual treasures, but for him to practise so elevating a profession as that of a priest simply because it is ancestral—without faith, without belief, merely as a mechanical process handed down from father to son—is not a conservation of virtue; it is really the prostitution of a noble profession which is no other than the service of religion.

8

8.1

Why does the Mahatma cling to the theory of everyone following his or her ancestral calling? He gives his reasons nowhere. But there must be some reason, although he does not care to avow it. Years ago, writing on "Caste versus Class" in his Young India,[12] he argued that the caste system was better than a class system on the ground that caste was the best possible adjustment for social stability. If that be the reason why the Mahatma clings to the theory of everyone following his or her ancestral calling, then he is clinging to a false view of social life.

8.2

Everybody wants social stability, and some adjustment must be made in the relationship between individuals and classes in order that stability may be had. But two things, I am sure, nobody wants. One thing nobody wants is a static relationship, something that is unalterable, something that is fixed for all times. Stability is wanted, but not at the cost of change when change is imperative. The second thing nobody wants is mere adjustment. Adjustment is wanted, but not at the sacrifice of social justice.

8.3

Can it be said that the adjustment of social relationships on the basis of caste—i.e., on the basis of each to his hereditary calling—avoids these two evils? I am convinced that it does not. Far from being the best possible adjustment, I have no doubt that it is of the worst possible kind, inasmuch as it offends against both the canons of social adjustment—namely, fluidity and equity.

9

9.1

Some might think that the Mahatma has made much progress, inasmuch as he now only believes in varna and does not believe in caste. It is true that there was a time when the Mahatma was a full- blooded and a blue-blooded sanatani Hindu.[13] He believed in the Vedas, the Upanishads, the puranas, and all that goes by the name of Hindu scriptures; and therefore, in avatars and rebirth. He believed in caste and defended it with the vigour of the orthodox.[14] He condemned the cry for inter-dining, inter-drinking, and intermarrying, and argued that restraints about inter-dining to a great extent "helped the cultivation of will-power and the conservation of a certain social virtue".

9.2

It is good that he has repudiated this sanctimonious nonsense and admitted that caste "is harmful both to spiritual and national growth", and maybe his son's marriage outside his caste has had something to do with this change of view. But has the Mahatma really progressed? What is the nature of the varna for which the Mahatma stands? Is it the Vedic conception as commonly understood and preached by Swami Dayanand Saraswati and his followers, the Arya Samajists? The essence of the Vedic conception of varna is the pursuit of a calling which is appropriate to one's natural aptitude. The essence of the Mahatma's conception of varna is the pursuit of one's ancestral calling, irrespective of natural aptitude.

9.3

What is the difference between caste and varna, as understood by the Mahatma? I find none. As defined by the Mahatma varna becomes merely a different name for caste, for the simple reason that it is the same in essence—namely, pursuit of one's ancestral calling. Far from making progress, the Mahatma has suffered retrogression. By putting this interpretation upon the Vedic conception of varna, he has
191 really made ridiculous what was sublime. While I reject the Vedic varnavyavastha for reasons given in the speech, I must admit that the Vedic theory of varna as interpreted by Swami Dayanand and some others is a sensible and an inoffensive thing. It did not admit birth as a determining factor in fixing the place of an individual in society. It only recognised worth.

9.4

The Mahatma's view of varna not only makes nonsense of the Vedic varna, but it makes it an abominable thing. Varna and caste are two very different concepts. Varna is based on the principle of each according to his worth, while caste is based on the principle of each according to his birth. The two are as distinct as chalk is from cheese. In fact, there is an antithesis between the two. If the Mahatma believes, as he does, in everyone following his or her ancestral calling, then most certainly he is advocating the caste system, and in calling it the varna system he is not only guilty of terminological inexactitude, but he is causing confusion worse confounded.

9.5

I am sure that all his confusion is due to the fact that the Mahatma has no definite and clear conception as to what is varna and what is caste, and as to the necessity of either for the conservation of Hinduism. He has said—and one hopes that he will not find some mystic reason to change his view—that caste is not the essence of Hinduism. Does he regard varna as the essence of Hinduism? One cannot as yet give any categorical answer.

9.6

Readers of his article on "Dr Ambedkar's Indictment" will answer "No." In that article he does not say that the dogma of varna is an essential part of the creed of Hinduism. Far from making varna the essence of Hinduism, he says "the essence of Hinduism is contained in its enunciation of one and only God as truth and its bold acceptance of ahimsa as the law of the human family".

9.7

But readers of his article in reply to Mr Sant Ram will say "Yes." In that article he says "How can a Muslim remain one if he rejects the Quran, or a Christian remain Christian if he rejects the Bible? If caste and varna are convertible terms, and if varna is an integral part of the shastras which define Hinduism, I do not know how a person who rejects caste, i.e., varna, can call himself a Hindu." Why this prevarication? Why does the Mahatma hedge? Whom does he want to please? Has the saint failed to sense the truth? Or does the politician stand in the way of the saint?

9.8

The real reason why the Mahatma is suffering from this confusion is probably to be traced to two sources. The first is the temperament of the Mahatma. He has in almost everything the simplicity of the child, with the child's capacity for selfdeception. Like a child, he can believe in anything he wants to believe in. We must therefore wait till such time as it pleases the Mahatma to abandon his faith in varna, as it has pleased him to abandon his faith in caste.

9.9

The second source of confusion is the double role which the Mahatma wants to play—of a Mahatma and a politician. As a Mahatma, he may be trying to spiritualise politics. Whether he has succeeded in it or not, politics have certainly commercialised him. A politician must know that society cannot bear the whole truth, and that he must not speak the whole truth; if he is speaking the whole truth it is bad for his politics. The reason why the Mahatma is always supporting caste and varna is because he is afraid that if he opposed them he would lose his place in politics. Whatever may be the source of this confusion the Mahatma must be told that he is deceiving himself, and also deceiving the people, by preaching caste under the name of varna.

10

10.1

The Mahatma says that the standards I have applied to test Hindus and Hinduism are too severe, and that judged by those standards every known living faith will probably fail. The complaint that my standards are high may be true. But the question is not whether they are high or whether they are low. The question is whether they are the right standards to apply. A people and their religion must be judged by social standards based on social ethics. No other standard would have any meaning, if religion is held to be a necessary good for the wellbeing of the people.

10.2

Now, I maintain that the standards I have applied to test Hindus and Hinduism are the most appropriate standards, and that I know of none that are better. The conclusion that every known religion would fail if tested by my standards may be true. But this fact should not give the Mahatma as the champion of Hindus and Hinduism a ground for comfort, any more than the existence of one madman should give comfort to another madman, or the existence of one criminal should give comfort to another criminal.

10.3

I would like to assure the Mahatma that it is not the mere failure of the Hindus and Hinduism which has produced in me the feelings of disgust and contempt with which I am charged. I realise that the world is a very imperfect world, and anyone who wants to live in it must bear with its imperfections.

10.4

But while I am prepared to bear with the imperfections and shortcomings of the society in which I may be destined to labour, I feel I should not consent to live in a society which cherishes wrong ideals, or a society which, having right ideals, will not consent to bring its social life into conformity with those ideals. If I am disgusted with Hindus and Hinduism, it is because I am convinced that they cherish wrong ideals and live a wrong social life. My quarrel with Hindus and Hinduism is not over the imperfections of their social conduct. It is much more fundamental. It is over their ideals.

11

11.1

Hindu society seems to me to stand in need of a moral regeneration which it is dangerous to postpone. And the question is, who can determine and control this moral regeneration? Obviously, only those who have undergone an intellectual regeneration and those who are honest enough to have the courage of their convictions born of intellectual emancipation. Judged by this standard, the Hindu leaders who count are, in my opinion, quite unfit for the task. It is impossible to say that they have undergone the preliminary intellectual regeneration. If they had undergone an intellectual regeneration, they would neither delude themselves in the simple way of the untaught multitude, nor would they take advantage of the primitive ignorance of others as one sees them doing.

11.2

Notwithstanding the crumbling state of Hindu society, these leaders will nevertheless unblushingly appeal to ideals of the past which have in every way ceased to have any connection with the present—ideals which, however suitable they might have been in the days of their origin, have now become a warning rather than a guide. They still have a mystic respect for the earlier forms which makes them disinclined— nay, opposed—to any examination of the foundations of their society. The Hindu masses are of course incredibly heedless in the formation of their beliefs. But so are the Hindu leaders. And what is worse is that these Hindu leaders become filled with an illicit passion for their beliefs when anyone proposes to rob them of their companionship.

11.3

The Mahatma is no exception. The Mahatma appears not to believe in thinking. He prefers to follow the saints. Like a conservative with his reverence for consecrated notions, he is afraid that if he once starts thinking, many ideals and institutions to which he clings will be doomed. One must sympathise with him. For every act of independent thinking puts some portion of an apparently stable world in peril.

11.4

But it is equally true that dependence on saints cannot lead us to know the truth. The saints are after all only human beings, and as Lord Balfour said, "the human mind is no more a truth-finding apparatus than the snout of a pig".[16] In so far as he does think, to me he really appears to be prostituting his intelligence to find reasons for supporting this archaic social structure of the Hindus. He is the most influential apologist of it and therefore the worst enemy of the Hindus.

11.5

Unlike the Mahatma, there are Hindu leaders who are not content merely to believe and follow. They dare to think, and act in accordance with the result of their thinking. But unfortunately they are either a dishonest lot, or an indifferent lot when it comes to the question of giving right guidance to the mass of the people. Almost every Brahmin has transgressed the rule of caste. The number of Brahmins who sell shoes is far greater than those who practise priesthood. Not only have the Brahmins given up their ancestral calling of priesthood for trading, but they have entered trades which are prohibited to them by the shastras. Yet how many Brahmins who break caste every day will preach against caste and against the shastras?

11.6

For one honest Brahmin preaching against caste and shastras because his practical instinct and moral conscience cannot support a conviction in them, there are hundreds who break caste and trample upon the shastras every day, but who are the most fanatic upholders of the theory of caste and the sanctity of the shastras. Why this duplicity? Because they feel that if the masses are emancipated from the yoke of caste, they would be a menace to the power and prestige of the Brahmins as a class. The dishonesty of this intellectual class, who would deny the masses the fruits of their thinking, is a most disgraceful phenomenon.

11.7

The Hindus, in the words of Matthew Arnold, are "wandering between two worlds, one dead, the other powerless to be born".[17] What are they to do? The Mahatma to whom they appeal for guidance does not believe in thinking, and can therefore give no guidance which can be said to stand the test of experience. The intellectual classes to whom the masses look for guidance are either too dishonest or too indifferent to educate them in the right direction. We are indeed witnesses to a great tragedy. In the face of this tragedy all one can do is to lament and say—such are thy leaders, O Hindus!

Notes

1. Same as 'runny nose'. The expression here means snivelling, "pitiful, whining" according to Sa Johnson's A Dictionary of the English Language.
2. Ambedkar is likely referring to Tilak's two-volume opus, Srimad Bhagavad Gita Rahasya, kno in short as Gita Rahasya and translated as The Esoteric Import of the Gita, in his own words. It was written when Tilak was imprisoned for six years on charges of sedition in Mandalay (Burma) from 1907 and first published in Marathi in June 1915. An English version translated by B.S. Sukthankar, which Ambedkar likely accessed, was published in 1935 by Tilak Bros in Poona. By then Gita Rahasya had been published in many Indian languages. This English edition features several pages of endorsements from a phalanx of leaders: Swami Vivekananda, Annie Besant, Madan Mohan Malaviya, Gopal Krishna Gokhale, Aurobindo Ghose and also Gandhi, who says Tilak's "masterwork commentary on the Gita is unsurpassed and will remain so for a long time to come" (xvi).
3. Eknath (1533—99) was a sixteenth-century Marathi sant of the Varkari tradition founded by Jnya (see Note 32 to AoC 2.22). Eknathi Bhagavat is a commentary on the eleventh canto of the Sanskrit Bhagavata Purana (a circa tenth-century puranic text—though scholars disagree on the dating—focused on Krishna and the Bhagvad Gita), in the form of abhangas, a Marathi verse form meaning unbroken, written in the ovi metre.
4. V. Shantaram made this film in 1935 on Eknath's life. The famous actor Bal Gandharv starred i role of Eknath.
5. (Antyajancha vital jyasi/ Gangasnane shuddhatva tyasi—Eknathi Bhagavat, a.28, o.191). This verse with reference to the source figures in the 1937 edition of AoC as a footnote at this point. This Marathi verse has been transcribed and translated by Debroy as: "Those among outcastes who are impure/ can be purified by bathing in the Ganga."

6. Despite his scepticism and rejection of the Bhakti movement and Bhakti saints, Ambedkar did recognise the agentive role of the 'Untouchable' Bhakti saints and dedicated The Untouchables: Who Were They and Why They Became Untouchable (1948/1990) thus: "Inscribed to the memory of Nandanar, Ravidas, Chokhamela—three renowned saints who were born among the Untouchables, and who by their piety and virtue won the esteem of all." Nandanar, however, was not a historical figure unlike Ravidas and Cokhamela. In the twelfth- century Tamil work Periya Puranam by Sekkilar, a hagiographical account of the sixty-three Tamil Saiva saints (Nayanmars) of whom only a handful were historical figures, the Paraiyar- born Nandanar is referred to as Thirunaali Povar. As Anushiya Ramaswamy (2010, 76) points out, Sekkilar shows Nandanar as "unquestioningly accepting the edicts of a caste-defined order, going so far as to willingly die in a ritualistic immolation at the gates of Chidambaram [Nataraja temple]". During the colonial-nationalist movement, the figure of Nandanar was resurrected. Gopalakrishna Bharathi, a Saivite poet-composer had published the Nandanar Charitram (The story of Nandanar) in 1861-2 which, during the early twentieth century, was adapted for stage as dance dramas. Later, five Tamil feature films were made on Nandanar— two silent films, in 1923 and 1930; and three talkies, in 1933, 1935 and 1942.
7. Ambedkar is also perhaps alluding to the fact that Gandhi often compared himself to the 'Bhang the caste among Untouchables forced into sweeping and scavenging work—and often announced that he cleaned the toilets in his ashrams. As far as Ambedkar is concerned, a saint or a Mahatma indulging in such performative gestures does not alter the beliefs of people as such. For an account of Gandhi's writings on manual scavengers, see Ramaswamy (2005, 8695); for a critique of Gandhi's approach to issues concerning sweepers and scavengers, see Prashad (1996, 2001).
8. The sentence in parenthesis is given as a footnote in AoC 1937. Ambedkar is referring to Brailsford's essay in the Aryan Path (April 1936, 166—9). Aryan Path was a journal published from Bombay by the Theosophical Society since 1930. Henry Noel Brailsford (1873-1958) was a British leftwing journalist and writer who started his career as a foreign correspondent during the war

in Crete. He continued to report from Paris and then Macedonia after the First World War. He supported the women's suffrage movement. He was made editor of The New Leader, the British Independent Labour Party newspaper, in 1922. After a seven-week tour of India he became a member of the India League, a British organisation spreading awareness about the ills of colonialism, and wrote Rebel India (1931), a treatise against colonial rule. In the essay Ambedkar is referring to, Brailsford offers a thesis "that our existing society can be made tolerable and even happy, without any fundamental change in its structure, if all of us, but more especially the privileged classes, can be induced to follow a high standard of morality in our dealings with our fellows. This was always the teaching of the Roman Catholic Church, though it used to forbid usury, and is still critical of high finance. Mr Gandhi has preached impressive sermons on these lines to landlords (especially in the United Provinces) and to industrial capitalists." Here, Brailsford comes to echo Gandhi's doctrine of trusteeship; for a critical analysis of this doctrine, see Roy's introduction to this volume.

9. When Ambedkar refers to "the one who is a faithful follower of his father", he is alluding to Gandhi's third son, Devdas Gandhi, who, in 1937, was appointed managing editor of Hindustan Times, the newspaper owned by G.D. Birla, a Marwari Bania industrialist who was a close associate and financier of Gandhi. In Delhi, Gandhi made the palatial Birla House his residence for over twenty-five years. (The Birla House was renamed Gandhi Smriti in 1971.) Gandhi's swarajist economic policies resulted in his colluding with the conservative industrialists of his time. For an analysis of Gandhi's relationship with G.D. Birla and other Swadeshi business houses, see Leah Renold (1994, 16-38). Gandhi's first son Harilal Gandhi was estranged from Gandhi and was not a 'faithful follower' of his since he embraced Islam on 29 May 1936, the same month and year in which AoC was first published. Harilal's conversion happened within a year after Ambedkar declared on 13 October 1935 in Yeola that he shall not die a Hindu and exhorted Untouchables to seek relief in a new religion. For an account of Harilal's life, see Chandulal Bhagubhai Dalal (2007).

10. Buddha Gaya or Bodh Gaya is the most sacred site in Buddhism, revered as the place where Buddha attained enlightenment. The

temple complex has for long been controlled by Brahmin mahants (priests). The Bodhgaya Temple Act, passed two years after India's independence, provides for a chairman and a committee of eight members, four Buddhist and four Hindu, "to manage and control the temple land and the properties appertaining thereto". Section 3(3) of the Act provides that "the District Magistrate of Gaya shall be the ex- officio Chairman of the Committee: provided that the State Government shall nominate a Hindu as Chairman of the Committee for the period during which the district Magistrate of Gaya is non-Hindu". For the uncanny resemblance this state of affairs has with the Conflict of Orders in ancient Rome, especially with the history of the process of appointment of consuls and tribunes, and the role of the Oracle at Delphi, see Note 27 at 2.20 and Note 36 at 3.5 of AoC. An amendment to allow non-Hindu chairmen in the committee was passed only in August 2013 by the Bihar Assembly.

11. A pir, meaning elder or saint, is the spiritual guide to the followers of Sufism, the mystic branch Islam. Sufis are organised into orders around a master who helps his disciples along the path of surrendering the ego in the worship of god. When Ambedkar says a Brahmin can be a priest to a pir, he is referring to the adaptability of the Brahmin which helps him survive any challenge. Elaborating on this in a sharper way in his critique of the Congress and Gandhi, he says (BAWS 9, 195): "I am quite aware that there are some protagonists of Hinduism who say that Hinduism is a very adaptable religion, that it can adjust itself to everything and absorb anything. I do not think many people would regard such a capacity in a religion as a virtue to be proud of just as no one would think highly of a child because it has developed the capacity to eat dung, and digest it. But that is another matter. It is quite true that Hinduism can adjust itself. The best example of its adjustability is the literary production called Allahupanishad which the Brahmins of the time of Akbar produced to give a place to his Din-e-llahi within Hinduism and to recognise it as the Seventh system of Hindu philosophy." For an understanding of Sufism, see the classic work of Annemarie Schimmel (1975) and the more recent work of Tanvir Anjum (2011).

12. Young India, a weekly in English, was founded and published from Bombay since 1915 by Indu Yagnik, along with Jamnadas

Dwarkadas and Shankerlal Banker. Yagnik also brought out Navajivan, a monthly in Gujarati. In 1919, Yagnik requested Gandhi, who had returned from South Africa, to take over as editor of Young India and Navajivan. Under Gandhi's editorship, Young India appeared since 7 May 1919 as a biweekly and from 7 September 1919 as a weekly from Sabarmati Ashram, Ahmedabad (Rajmohan Gandhi, 2007, 211). Gandhi published Young India till he founded the Harijan in 1932. Ambedkar here is referring to Gandhi's piece dated 29 December 1920, where he argues why caste is better than class: "The beauty of the caste system is that it does not base itself upon distinctions of wealth-possessions. Money, as history has proved, is the greatest disruptive force in the world. Even the sacredness of family ties is not safe against the pollution of wealth, says Shankaracharya. Caste is but an extension of the principle of the family. Both are governed by blood and heredity ... Caste does not connote superiority or inferiority. It simply recognises different outlooks and corresponding modes of life. But it is no use denying the fact that a sort of hierarchy has been evolved in the caste system, but it cannot be called the creation of the Brahmins" (CWMG 22, 154—5).

13. Gandhi on his being a sanatani: "The friend next asked me for a definition of a sanatani Hindu a said: 'Could a sanatani Hindu Brahmin interdine with a Hindu non-Brahmin although the latter may be a non-vegetarian?' My definition of a sanatani Brahmin is: He who believes in the fundamental principles of Hinduism is a sanatani Hindu. And the fundamental principles of Hinduism are absolute belief in truth (satya) and ahimsa (non-violence)." Reported in The Hindu, 23 March 1925, from a speech in Madras at the height of the Non-Brahmin Movement in the Madras Presidency. In another speech in Calcutta, around the same time, Gandhi says: "Let the sanatani Hindus understand from me who claims to be a sanatani Hindu. I do not ask you to interdine with anybody; I do not ask you to exchange your daughters with the Untouchables or with anybody, but I do ask you to remove this curse [of untouchability] so that you may not put him beyond the pale of service." From Amrita Bazar Patrika, 2 May 1925. Anil Nauriya, however, makes the case (2006, 1835) that Gandhi's views on varna changed in the mid-1940s and that he came to denounce varnashrama: "Gandhi

incrementally unfurled a critique of the fourfold varna order, taking the concept of such an order in the end, by the mid- 1940s, to vanishing point." On such exercises in 'cherry picking', see Roy's introduction to this volume.

14. David Hardiman writes (2004, 126) that during the South African years, Gandhi "had appeared have little time for the caste system. He had been expelled from his own Baniya sub-caste for travelling overseas—considered a 'polluting' act at that time—and had never sought to gain readmission to the caste. In 1909, he condemned the caste system and caste tyranny. On his return to India he adopted a much softer line on the question. He denied that the caste system had harmed India, arguing that it was no more than a form of labour division, similar to occupational divisions all over the world. It was in fact superior to class divisions, 'which were based on wealth primarily'. He also believed that reform could be brought about through caste organisations."
15. Ambedkar is once again citing Gandhi from his Young India piece of 29 December 1920: "Inter dining has never been known to promote brotherhood in any special sense. But the restraints about interdining have to a great extent helped the cultivation of will-power and the conservation of certain social virtues" (CWMG 22, 156).
16. Lord (Arthur James) Balfour was a British conservative politician who served as Prime Minist between 1902 and 1905 and as Foreign Secretary between 1916 and 1919. It is not clear where Lord Balfour spoke these words, but there are other citations of this from the same period, each slightly differing in detail. The World Review (1936, 67) cites Balfour thus: "Lord Balfour has wisely said that 'The human brain is as much an organ for seeking food as the pig's snout.' After all, the human brain is only an enlarged piece of the spinal column, whose first function is to sense danger and preserve life."
17. These lines are from the poem "Stanzas from the Grande Chartreuse" by Matthew Arnold (1822 88), English poet and literary critic, reflecting the inner conflict of the Victorian era between scientific progress on the one hand, and religion, identity and values on the other. Ambedkar cites Arnold in "Castes in India" (1916) as well, written during his years at Columbia University It is possible that

Ambedkar often turned to Arnold thanks to his mentor Dewey, who was fond of quoting him. According to S. Morris Eames (1969, xxxvii), Dewey's essay "Poetry and Philosophy" (1890) begins with a long epigraph from Arnold. Eames says: "Dewey is appreciative of many of the insights of Matthew Arnold, and in later years he turns again and again to ideas he attributed to this poet and critic. Arnold once wrote that 'poetry is a criticism of life', and while Dewey thinks that poetry is more than this, he was influenced by Arnold's view in transferring it into philosophy, for he later writes that philosophy 'is inherently criticism', and in his own method makes philosophy 'a criticism of criticisms'." This idea is also echoed by the Italian political thinker Antonio Gramsci (1891-1937), a contemporary of Ambedkar: "The crisis consists precisely in the fact that the old is dying and the new cannot be born; in this interregnum a great variety of morbid symptoms appear" (1971, 276).

A Note on the Poona Pact

S. Anand

If the Communal Award of 16 August 1932 was a victory of sorts for those who sought to take social difference seriously in India, the Poona Pact of 24 September 1932 was a defeat. At a time of urgent political and ideological contestation over the future of India, the pact abruptly came in the way of more ambitious ways of fashioning a democracy that would suit a subcontinent made up essentially of caste, religious, regional and linguistic minorities, what B.R. Ambedkar termed a "congeries of communities".[1] This was a time when Ambedkar, with radical foresight, was trying to stymie the adoption of a first- past-the-post system, which he feared in the Indian context would result in a Hindu communal majority parading as a political majority. M.K. Gandhi, on the other hand, opposed special representation to every other community except the Muslims and the Sikhs. He argued that separate electorates "would simply vivisect and disrupt" Hinduism, and suggested that the Communal Award "will create a division in Hinduism which I cannot possibly look forward to with any satisfaction whatsoever".[2] It was to oppose the political rights granted to the Untouchables by the Communal Award that Gandhi took a dramatic and coercive step—a fast unto death on 20 September 1932 that culminated in the Poona Pact only four days later.

Indian academia, its intelligentsia and the political establishment have remained, for the most part, indifferent to the complex workings of both the Communal Award and the Poona Pact. (The few exceptions have mostly been followers of the Dalit movement.[3]) In nationalist histories, 207 the Communal Award, which granted separate electorates not just to Untouchables but to Muslims, Sikhs, Christians, Anglo- Indians, Europeans, landlords, labourers and traders, continues to be depicted as unambiguously divisive. Since Annihilation of Caste is in part a response to the disappointment Ambedkar felt over the Poona Pact, it is important to understand what it practically meant. What led to the Communal Award? What was the thrust of Gandhi's opposition to it? What were the terms of the Poona Pact? Did the Congress honour these terms? The answers to these questions also hold the key to understanding Ambedkar's vehement attack on not just the caste system, but on Hinduism itself and its founding texts, in Annihilation of Caste.[4] Indeed Ambedkar was so devastated that he also went on to write—thirteen years after the Poona Pact—the strongest indictment of the pact, Gandhi and the Congress in What Congress and Gandhi Have Done to the Untouchables.

The first Round Table Conference (RTC) was convened in London by the Labour government of Ramsay MacDonald from 12 November 1930 to 19 January 1931 to discuss the future constitution of India. Since Gandhi had initiated the Civil Disobedience Movement in 1930, the Congress abstained from the first round, which was eventually attended by Ambedkar and Rettamalai Srinivasan representing the Untouchables, M.A. Jinnah (among others) representing the Muslims, and representatives of various minority communities as well as of the princely states. However, by the time of the second RTC, Lord Irwin came to an agreement with the Congress, and it decided to attend the conference (from 7 September 1931 to 1 December 1931), with Gandhi as its representative.

At the conference, Gandhi impugned the leaders of the Muslim, Sikh, Untouchable and Christian communities, ridiculing their claims to self-representation. While he eventually came around to accepting the communal scheme of representation for Sikhs and Muslims, Gandhi was particularly opposed to Ambedkar, who made a case for "separate electorates" for the Depressed Classes. What for Ambedkar was a matter of securing the political rights of the Untouchables was for Gandhi a matter of religion. In a letter to Sir Samuel Hoare, then Secretary of State for India, on 11 March 1932, he said: "For me the question of these classes is predominantly moral and religious. The political aspect, important though it is, dwindles into insignificance compared to the moral and religious issue."[5]

Ambedkar's report on the seriousness with which Gandhi attended the conference is worth quoting at length:

I am sure I am not exaggerating or misrepresenting facts when I say that the Congress point of view at the Round Table Conference was that the Congress was the only party in India and that nobody else counted and that the British should settle with the Congress only. This was the burden of Mr Gandhi's song at the Round Table Conference. He was so busy in establishing his own claim to recognition by the British as the dictator of India that he forgot altogether that the important question was not with whom the settlement should be made but what were to be the terms of that settlement. As to the terms of the setdement, Mr Gandhi was quite unequal to the task. When he went to London he had forgotten that he would have before him not those who go to him to obtain his advice and return with his blessings but persons who would treat him as a lawyer treats a witness in the box. Mr Gandhi also forgot that he was going to a political conference. He went there as though he was going to a Vaishnava Shrine singing Narsi Mehta's songs. When I think of the whole affair I am wondering if any nation had ever sent a representative to negotiate the terms of a national settlement who was more unfit than Mr Gandhi.

Gandhi held on to the view that the Congress was the sole representative of all Indians. In an article in Harijan on 21 October 1939, tellingly captioned "The Fiction of Majority", he wrote with the conviction that only a Mahatma can summon:

I know that many have been angry with me for claiming an exclusive right for the Congress to speak for the people of India as a whole. It is not an arrogant pretension. It is explicit in the first article of the Congress. It wants and works for independence for the whole of India. It speaks neither for majority nor minority. It seeks to represent all Indians without any distinction. Therefore those who oppose it should not count, if the claim for independence is admitted. Those who support the claim simply give added strength to the Congress claim ... In other words and in reality, so far as India is concerned, there can only be political parties and no majority or minority communities. The cry of the tyranny of the majority is a fictitious cry.

In this piece, Gandhi goes on to mock all claims to minority rights, saying Brahmins and zamindars (landlords) too could claim the minority tag.

Notwithstanding Gandhi's opposition, the Communal Award of 16 August 1932 allotted, among other things, separate electorates and two votes to the Depressed Classes/ Untouchables for twenty years, though Ambedkar had sought them only for ten years. Clause 9 of the Award read:

Members of the 'Depressed Classes' qualified to vote will vote in a general constituency. In view of the fact that for a considerable period these classes would be unlikely, by this means alone, to secure any adequate representation in the Legislature, a number of special seats will be assigned to them ... These seats will be filled by election from special constituencies in which only members of the 'Depressed Classes' electorally qualified will be entitled to vote. Any person voting in such a special constituency will, as stated above, be also entitled to vote in a general constituency. It is intended that these constituencies should be formed in selected areas where the Depressed Classes are most numerous, and that, except in Madras, they should not cover the whole area of the Province.

In these double-member constituencies (DMCs), one member was to be selected from among Untouchables (or Adivasis/Scheduled Tribes as the case may be), and one from among the Hindus.[9] This meant, first, that Untouchables, and only Untouchables, would choose their representatives to legislatures. Second, they would be able to cast a second ballot to have a say in who among the caste Hindus was best suited—or least inimical—to represent Untouchable interests in a legislative body. Such safeguards were necessary, argued Ambedkar, since not only were Untouchables outnumbered b y savarnas (caste Hindus), sometimes to the tune of "one to ten", they were also physically vulnerable to attacks by caste Hindus during elections—the kind of violence that continues to take place in most parts of India even today. Since the Untouchables did not enjoy civil, economic or religious rights on a par with the caste Hindus, and they were widely and routinely stigmatised, Ambedkar believed that a mere right to vote would do them no good, and that they would be subject to the manipulations and machinations of Hindus. The double vote, with the right to exclusively elect their own representatives, would ensure that the savarnas and the rest of society came to regard Untouchables as worthy of respect and dignity. Indeed, Untouchables would become politically consequential citizens—Dalits.

Gandhi's response to the Communal Award was to deploy the most powerful weapon in his arsenal. He announced that he would fast—unto death—until the Award was revoked. The nation flew into panic. Gandhi's lieutenant, C. Rajagopalachari, suggested that the "20th of September should be observed as a day of fasting and prayer all over India".[10]

The British government said it would revoke the Award only if Ambedkar agreed. At first, Ambedkar asked Gandhi to weigh in the truth: "If the Mahatma chooses to ask the Depressed Classes to make a choice between Hindu faith and possession of political power, I am quite sure that the Depressed Classes will choose political power and save the Mahatma from self-immolation."[11] Ambedkar was making a point he had always made—about his unease with being told that the Untouchables belong to the 'Hindu' fold. "I'm not a part of the whole. I am a part apart," he was to say as a member of the Bombay Legislative Assembly in 1939.[12]

As Ambedkar stood his ground, the British Prime Minister Ramsay MacDonald tried to reassure Gandhi that the provisions of the Communal Award did not in any way divide the Depressed Classes and the Hindus. In a letter dated 8 September 1932, he explained to Gandhi that "the Depressed Classes will remain part of the Hindu community and will vote with the Hindu electorate on an equal footing". MacDonald pointed out that in the "limited number of special constituencies" meant to safeguard the "rights and interests" of the Untouchables, "the Depressed Classes will not be deprived of their votes in the general Hindu constituencies, but will have two votes in order that their membership of the Hindu community should remain unimpaired". He further argued that such safeguards were not applicable to Muslims who "cannot vote or be a candidate in a general constituency, whereas any electorally qualified member of the Depressed Classes can vote in and stand for the general constituency".[13]

On 19 September, one day before the commencement of Gandhi's fast, Ambedkar said, "I can never consent to deliver my people bound hand and foot to the Caste Hindus for generations to come." He described Gandhi's epic fast as an "extreme form of coercion", a "foul and filthy act", and a "vow of self-immolation".[14]

Gandhi nevertheless went ahead with his religious "vow". Almost all the leaders of the national movement rallied behind him, and by implication, against Ambedkar. Gandhi's son Devdas publicly begged Ambedkar to save his father's life. Pleading with the Mahatma to relent, Ambedkar pointed out that should Gandhi die, it would "result in nothing but terrorism by his followers against the Depressed Classes all over the country".[15] Vulnerable and hated and living on the margins of a society that routinely resorted to collective punishment against them, this was not a chance Ambedkar could, in good conscience, afford to take on behalf of the Untouchables. He had been placed in an impossible position, and forced into a decision that would haunt him for the rest of his life. On 24 September 1932, Ambedkar gave in and signed the Poona Pact as the principal signatory on behalf of the Depressed Classes, while the right-wing Hindu Mahasabha leader, Pandit Madan Mohan Malaviya, represented Gandhi and the Hindus. Gandhi did not sign the pact.

Under the Poona Pact, Untouchables had to give up their separate electorate and be part of joint electorates with Hindus. They also had to give up the unique political weapon Ambedkar had won for them—the second vote that would give them a say in the election of caste-Hindu candidates in their constituency. All that remained for Scheduled Castes was a reserved seat whose holder would be selected by the general population. The Scheduled Caste representative would, in effect, be selected by the very caste-Hindu majority that had already proved its hostility to Scheduled Caste political aspirations.

What was the immediate fallout of the 1932 arrangement? Once the provisions of the Poona Pact were incorporated into the Government of India Act of 1935—the Constitution of British India— elections to the provincial legislatures took place in February 1937. This was to be the first test of the efficacy of the Poona Pact, whose key provision lay in Clause 2:

Election to these seats shall be by joint electorates subject, however, to the following procedure:

All the members of the Depressed Classes, registered in the general electoral roll in a constituency, will form an electoral college, which will elect a panel of four candidates belonging to the Depressed Classes for each of such reserved seats by the method of the single vote; the four persons getting the highest number of votes in such primary election shall be candidates for election by the general electorate.

While the novel concept of 'primaries' was thus introduced for the first time in India, the vague wording left a lot to interpretation. The seemingly innocuous "panel of four", Ambedkar felt, could be misused and abused. Should the panel have a minimum of four members or a maximum of four candidates? And what would be the method of voting in the final election? To address such questions a committee, headed by Sir Laurie Hammond, was constituted. According to Ambedkar, the Hindus maintained that the panel of four was intended to be a minimum. This meant that if four candidates were not forthcoming or available, there could be no primary election, and thus there would be no election for the reserved seat. In his deposition before the Hammond Committee, Ambedkar asserted that four in the Poona Pact meant "not more than four", and not "not less than four". Ambedkar believed that a baggy panel of four meant the Hindus would be at an advantage "to capture the seat for an election of such a representative of the Untouchable candidate who would be their nominee and who would be most willing to be the tool of the Hindus".[17] That is, the Hindus would ensure a weak and pliable Untouchable candidate in the panel, and further 214.

on elect such a person. Suppose there was no panel, and only Untouchables got to decide who would represent them, such a candidate, according to Ambedkar, "would be the staunchest representative of the Untouchables and worst from the standpoint of the Hindus".

Furthermore, the representative of the Hindus deposing to the Hammond Committee claimed that the "compulsory distributive" vote was the most appropriate, while Ambedkar argued for the "cumulative" system of voting. Under compulsory distributive vote, "the elector has also as many votes as there are seats, but he can give only one vote to any one candidate". This means the Untouchable voter cannot cast all four votes to one favoured candidate. This could happen under the cumulative system, where "the elector has as many votes as there are seats" and "may give them all to one candidate or he may distribute them over two or more candidates as he may desire".[19] Ambedkar argued that under the distributive mechanism the possibilities of manipulation were higher:

Their main object was to flood the election to the seat reserved for the Untouchables in the joint electorate by using the surplus votes of the Hindus in favour of the Untouchable candidate who happens to be their nominee. The object was to outnumber the Untouchable voters and prevent them from electing their own nominee. This cannot be done unless the surplus votes of the Hindu voters were diverted from the Hindu candidate towards the Untouchable candidates. There is a greater chance of the diversion of these surplus votes under the distributive system than there is under the cumulative system.

In Ambedkar's reckoning, if the caste Hindus were given a clearer choice under the cumulative system, they would prefer to fight their battles with one another—a caste-Hindu voter could give all votes to his favourite caste-Hindu candidate as against rival caste-Hindu candidates, and leave the Untouchable candidates untouched. But if they were forced to give only one vote per candidate, in the distributive system, their hatred for a radical Untouchable candidate would outweigh, in their minds, the preference for a second, third or fourth caste-Hindu candidate.

After hearing out all views, the Hammond Committee ruled that the number four in the primaries panel is "neither a maximum nor a minimum, but an optimum". It further ruled that "if there is only one candidate as the result of the primary election, or on account of subsequent withdrawals, that candidate should be returned unopposed for the reserved seat at the final election".[21] Another crucial decision was that the "primary election should take place two months before the final election", thus providing ample scope for the caste Hindus to back their preferred Untouchable candidate.

The tug of war since the Round Table Conferences was about who would have the 'final say'. The caste Hindus wanted to have the final say in the lives of Untouchables even in the new paradigms of electoral democracy and representation. However, given that they were a persecuted minority, the Untouchables—represented by Ambedkar—wanted to reverse this historical logic and have a final say in the lives of caste Hindus, the majority community For the Hindus, led by Gandhi, this radical idea was anathema. Ambedkar reflects on this conundrum in Annihilation of Caste by comparing the Communal Award with the republican constitution of Rome, where he argues that the patricians and the plebeians "formed two distinct castes". The plebeians "never could get a plebeian consul who could be said to be a strong man, and who could act independently of the patrician consul". Ambedkar likens the manner in which the plebeians lose their rights to how Untouchables lose out in the Poona Pact—the caste Hindus and patricians offer some concessions but retain a final say in the lives of Untouchables and plebeians respectively.[22]

Although Ambedkar conceded that the number of seats Untouchables got after the Poona Pact had almost doubled compared to what he had bargained for in the Communal Award,[23] he was alert to its true import. Ambedkar lamented the loss of the "priceless privilege" of the double vote whose "value as a political weapon was beyond reckoning":

No caste-Hindu candidate could have dared to neglect the Untouchable in his constituency or be hostile to their interest if he was made dependent upon the votes of the Untouchables. Today the Untouchables have a few more seats than were given to them by the Communal Award. But this is all that they have. Every other member is indifferent, if not hostile. If the Communal Award with its system of double voting had remained the Untouchables would have had a few seats less but every other member would have been a member for the Untouchables. The increase in the number of seats for the Untouchables is no increase at all and was no recompense for the loss of separate electorates and the double vote.[24]

At the heart of Ambedkar's approach to democracy was the question of how to ensure that all minorities—especially, but not only, the Untouchables—could successfully bargain for adequate protections. Democracy, in theory, was premised on the idea of 'one person, one value' and hence 'one person, one vote'. But Untouchables, treated as lesser humans, were not accorded the same value as Touchables. To make democracy substantive in a caste-differentiated society, therefore, it required modification. In such a redesigned democracy, the value of a devalued Untouchable had to be deliberately raised through special provisions such as the double vote or the adoption of the principle of reservation, or both.

In the 1937 elections, there were 151 reserved seats25 from which only Untouchables could be elected. The Congress won 217 seventy-eight of these, and in Ambedkar's words, it "left only 73 seats to be filled by true and independent representatives of the Untouchables" (BAWS 9, 92). For, he argued, the majority of seventy-eight seats won by the Congress "were won with the help of Hindu votes and they do not therefore in any way represent the Scheduled Castes" (BAWS 9, iii). Significantly, the Congress, despite its financial muscle, lost out to non Congress Untouchable candidates in Bombay and Bengal, where the Dalit movement was strong. Ambedkar formed the Independent Labour Party only five months before the

February 1937 election, despite which the ILP "obtained an astonishing degree of success. Out of the 15 seats assigned to the Scheduled Castes in Bombay Presidency it captured 13 and in addition it won 2 general seats".[26]

More crucially, according to Ambedkar, the Congress provincial ministries across the country decided not to offer any cabinet posts to a single one of the seventy-eight Untouchable legislators. At the Round Table Conferences, Ambedkar had "pressed the claim of the Untouchables for the recognition of their right to representation in the Cabinet with the same emphasis" as he had done for "the recognition of their right to representation in the Legislature".[27] When Narayan Bhaskar Khare,[28] the Prime Minister of the Congress ministry in the Central Provinces, formed a Cabinet with R.G. Agnibhoj, an Untouchable, as one of his ministers, the Congress Working Committee met in Wardha and passed a resolution on 26 July 1938 condemning Khare. Ambedkar says:

Dr Khare openly said that according to Mr Gandhi the act of indiscipline consisted in the inclusion of an Untouchable in the Ministry. Dr Khare also said that Mr Gandhi told him that it was wrong on his part to have raised such aspirations and ambitions in the Untouchables and it was such an act of bad judgement that he would never forgive him. This statement was repeatedly made by Dr Khare from platforms. Mr Gandhi has never contradicted it.

In 1942, an Untouchable member of the Congress, having attended the All-India Scheduled Castes Conference, wrote a letter to Gandhi and signed it as "Five Questions by a Harijan M.L.A." He sought to know from Gandhi if in the future constitution of India he would ensure the representation of Untouchables by agreeing "to fix the five seats from a Panchayat Board upwards to the State Council on population basis"; if, "in view of the backwardness of the Harijans", Gandhi would advise the government to ensure that executive posts in the "Local Boards and Municipal Councils be held on communal rotation, so as to enable the Harijans to become Presidents and Chairmen"; if he would advise Congress ministries to ensure that Scheduled Caste legislators are made Cabinet ministers; and if he could "fix some percentage of seats for Harijans from District Congress Committee upwards to the Working Committee of the Congress". Gandhi's reply, given on 2 August 1942 in his mouthpiece Harijan, resorted to the logic of meritocracy used often by those opposed to any form of affirmative action:

> The principle is dangerous. Protection of its neglected classes should not be carried to an extent which will harm them and harm the country. A cabinet minister should be a topmost man commanding universal confidence. A person after he has secured a seat in an elected body should depend upon his intrinsic merit and popularity to secure coveted positions.[30]

Ambedkar also saw a pattern in the manner in which the Congress oversaw the selection of non-Brahmin and Untouchable candidates:

> From candidates who came from high caste Hindus, such as Brahmins and the allied communities, those with the highest qualifications were selected. In the case of the Non-Brahmins those with low qualifications were preferred to those with higher qualifications. And in the case of the Untouchables those with little or no qualifications were selected in preference to those who had.

He came to the conclusion that "the Congress sucked the juice out of the Poona Pact and threw the rind in the face of the Untouchables".[32]

The ghost of the Poona Pact was to haunt the man who knew how the caste Hindus would use its logic to ensure the defeat of the best of Dalits.[33] Thus the man who from 1946 to 1950 piloted the drafting of the Indian Constitution was humiliated twice at the hustings in independent India, both times by less able candidates that the Congress fielded. In the first ever polls to the Lok Sabha in 1951, contesting on the ticket of his party, the Scheduled Castes Federation, from the reserved part of the double-member Bombay North constituency, Ambedkar was defeated by 14,374 votes by Narayan Sadoba Kajrolkar of the Congress. The Congress deliberately fielded a candidate who was a Chambhar, the largest Untouchable caste after the Mahars in the region. He was also a known opponent of Ambedkar, a Mahar.[34] Kajrolkar had opposed Ambedkar on the Communal Award as well as over his call for conversion, saving "we are shocked at the advice given to us, Harijans, by our veteran leader Dr Ambedkar, to abandon the Hindu religion ... It breaks our hearts to see... [that] Dr Ambedkar who gave us a prominent lead in the past, should ask us to commit suicide by abandoning our religion."[35] When Ambedkar tried his luck in the 1954 by-election from Bhandara, Maharashtra, he lost again, this time to another Congress candidate, Bhaurao Borkar, someone who earlier used to organise workers for the Scheduled Castes Federation, the party founded and led by Ambedkar.

Today, India boasts of having a system of political reservations that ensures that Scheduled Castes and Scheduled Tribes are elected to all legislative bodies—from the panchayat upwards—in proportion to their share in the population. In the case of the Lok Sabha, the Lower House of Parliament, of its 543 seats, seventy-nine are reserved for Dalits, and forty-one for Adivasis.

However, Ambedkar, and Dalits today, would have been happier with more juice and less rind.